W9-ACS-881

MILTON STUDIES

XI

MILTON STUDIES
James D. Simmonds, Editor

MILTON STUDIES

STUDIES

XI ᕙᕦ ᕙᕦ ᕙᕦ

The Presence of Milton

B. Rajan
Guest Editor

WITHDRAWN

UNIVERSITY OF PITTSBURGH PRESS

BURG
PR
3579
. M5
V. 11
1978

MILTON STUDIES

is published annually by the University of Pittsburgh Press as a forum for
Milton scholarship and criticism. Articles submitted for publication may
be biographical; they may interpret some aspect of Milton's writings; or
they may define literary, intellectual, or historical contexts—by studying
the work of his contemporaries, the traditions which affected his thought
and art, contemporary political and religious movements, his influence on
other writers, or the history of critical response to his work.

Manuscripts should be upwards of 3,000 words in length and should
conform to the *MLA Style Sheet*. Manuscripts and editorial correspondence should be addressed to James D. Simmonds, Department of English, University of Pittsburgh, Pittsburgh, Pa. 15260.

Milton Studies does not review books.

Within the United States, *Milton Studies* may be ordered from the
University of Pittsburgh Press, Pittsburgh, Pa. 15260.

Overseas orders should be addressed to Feffer and Simons, Inc., 100
Park Avenue, New York, N.Y. 10017, U.S.A.

A slightly modified version of "On Looking Into Pope's Milton" by
Barbara K. Lewalski first appeared in *Etudes Anglaises*, no. 4 (1974). Used
by permission of Librairie Marcel Didier, Paris.

Library of Congress Catalog Card Number 69-12335
ISBN 0-8229-3174-5 (Volume I) (out of print)
ISBN 0-8229-3194-x (Volume II)
ISBN 0-8229-3218-0 (Volume III)
ISBN 0-8229-3244-x (Volume IV)
ISBN 0-8229-3272-5 (Volume V)
ISBN 0-8229-3288-1 (Volume VI)
ISBN 0-8229-3305-5 (Volume VII)
ISBN 0-8229-3310-1 (Volume VIII)
ISBN 0-8229-3329-2 (Volume IX)
ISBN 0-8229-3356-x (Volume X)
ISBN 0-8229-3373-x (Volume XI)
US ISSN 0076-8820
Published by the University of Pittsburgh Press, Pittsburgh, Pa. 15260
Copyright © 1978, University of Pittsburgh Press
All rights reserved
Feffer and Simons, Inc., London
Manufactured in the United States of America

Burg.
78- C 6073

CONTENTS

PREFACE

THREE OF the essays in this volume began as papers that were read to commemorate Milton's tercentenary at a conference of the International Association of University Professors of English at Los Angeles in 1974. Professor Irene Samuel was responsible for arranging these papers. Her contribution to the making of this book is gratefully acknowledged.

INTRODUCTION:
THE VARIETIES OF PRESENCE

THE SIX essays in this book are offered as a beginning. Since the publication of Raymond Dexter Havens's *The Influence of Milton on English Poetry* just over fifty-five years ago, the only book to explore this intimidating subject has been Joseph Wittreich's *Milton and the Line of Vision*. Wittreich's collection of essays, as the title suggests, examines only one element, though an important one, in the Miltonic continuity. There is need for a reassessment which takes advantage both of changing understandings of Milton and of changing understandings of the nature of influence itself. This book is put forward as an initial contribution to such a reassessment.

This book is titled *The Presence of Milton* because the word "influence" has become too strongly attached to verbal emulation or reminiscence. We need a term that is ample enough to accommodate the many forms of relationship that arise from and declare the Miltonic continuity. We also need a term that will take account of strategies of disavowal and avoidance that acknowledge the impact of Milton's work even while seeming formally to dismiss it. "Presence" may not be the ideal word for such uses, but it is at least a relatively new word that can be given its content by the evidence.

The six contributors to this volume have looked at the encounters of individual authors with Milton. Each, in considering his or her author, has outlined a different form of relationship, a different styling of the response to a dominant predecessor or, in Dryden's case, to a senior contemporary. The manifestations of Milton's presence are by no means exhausted in the essays collected here; but the variety brought together should be sufficient to warn us that while a general theory of influence is by no means impossible, the existing body of theorizing must be considerably refined if it is to engage even the cases before us.

Dryden and Milton were contemporaries, as Earl Miner reminds us, and the interchange between them might well be along the lines worked out for our century in Richard Ellmann's *Eminent Domain*. Dryden's allusions to Milton are not exercises in the uses of the past but efforts to define the language of contemporaneity, to evolve cooperatively and to share a poetic speech that can discourse eloquently on more than one subject. Perhaps it is because such a language has been brought into being that Pope can make use of those exactly controlled displacements which Barbara Lewalski so tellingly enumerates. In Pope's translations of Homer, the Miltonic allusions and the Miltonic turns of speech define the elevation that is necessary if the classical epic is to be successfully Englished. In *The Essay on Man* the displacements measure the difference in magnitude between a religious and an ethical universe. In *The Rape of the Lock* the misapplications and the incongruities of scale characterize the mock-heroic with a precision that is only possible because a Miltonic presence and a Miltonic language exist. In *The Dunciad* the displacement is demonic, inviting us to pass beyond misapplication to an understanding of the true dimensions of dullness. In each of these cases Pope's use of Milton characterizes and works out with exactness the decorum of his specific undertaking. Such exactness is only possible when an accepted standard of measurement is firmly in being.

The purpose of a "concern with speech," Eliot tells us, is "to lead the mind to aftersight and foresight," and this may be why the Miltonic style seems so cogently related to what has come to be called the Miltonic vision. Blake's relationship with Milton, as Joseph Wittreich shows us, is one of creative collaboration in the attainment of that vision. To share in writing the next chapter in the journey of consciousness, the predecessor must renounce that which is backward-looking in himself, must purify himself to enter contemporaneity. In the resultant partnership, the predecessor comes to represent the force of continuity in the mind's creative history. Some may consider this misprision of a kind, dominated less by anxiety than by a sense of destiny resolute enough to make creative use of what it finds creative in Milton. But misprision scarcely describes Blake's huge elaboration of the myth of dismemberment and reconstitution, of which the Osiris image in *Areopagitica* provides an eloquent and seminal example. We could go further and suggest that the "Osiris principle" of the search and the "Urania principle" of vision are placed by Milton in relationships which continue to fascinate English poetry after him. These principles were present and, for that matter, co-present in poetry before Milton. But Milton does advance and perhaps even crucially formulate the language of engagement between these principles.

Blake's uniquely strong response to the Miltonic presence is not without its share of verbal reminiscence, but it is not a response which verbal reminiscence dominates. It deserves to be entered as a remonstrance against those who continue to identify the extent of influence with the extent of allusiveness. Wordsworth is, of course, lavish with verbal invocations of Milton, and the obvious reflections are perhaps at this stage less interesting than the subtler patterns of commentary that can also be traced. Nevertheless, it might be more profitable to give some attention to the structural presence of *Paradise Lost* in *The Prelude*—if only to put it to future students of this subject that structural presence may be no less important than verbal presence, or the presence of central understandings to which Milton has given a unique formative impact. It is not simply that an early line of *The Prelude* echoes a closing line of *Paradise Lost*, suggesting that the end of Milton's poem is also the beginning of ourselves. The new chapter remembers the old one, and it is no accident that the declaration of belief in man in *The Prelude* comes at the same structural point as the creation of man in Milton's epic. It follows an account of the Paradise of Helvellyn as sustainedly Miltonic as anything Wordsworth wrote; and it is accompanied by a profoundly ambivalent invocation of an image from the eleventh book of *Paradise Lost* when Michael descends to tell Adam of his expulsion from Paradise. Light comes from a quarter where we do not expect it, and man can be other than the record of his destructiveness indicates; but the account of the French Revolution will follow, and the allusion is proleptic to at least this degree. Moreover, the structural presence so far established invites us to relate the French Revolution to the Fall. A formal change of argument reminiscent of the opening of the ninth book of *Paradise Lost* is a further encouragement to take this route. The ascent of Snowdon can now be structurally joined to Adam's ascent of the highest hill of Paradise with both poems coming to related understandings discerned from related summits. The heart of creative change lies not in the reformation of external institutions but in an inward renewal that rejoins us to the divine will or to the truths of nature through the forms of the imagination.

The Romantics may have seen Milton's Satan predominantly

as the Promethean hero or as creative energy warring with institutionalized reason, but these findings, though widely endorsed, were not unanimous. In documenting Wordsworth's and Coleridge's consistent association of Napoleon with the paradigms of tyranny offered by Satan and Nimrod, Edna Newmeyer draws attention to a minority view of some importance. The same association can lead to different judgments and Hazlitt, as Professor Newmeyer indicates, found Napoleon-Satan heroic. These complications suggest that a reappraisal of the Romantic response to Satan is due. In particular the view, brought about largely by the problem of Satan, that *Paradise Lost* consists of two poems—an establishment exercise and a true poem of the imagination that for the sensitive reader overthrows the nominal one—deserves to be traced in some of its ramifications. Since the poem at odds with itself or doubting itself is not an uncommon Romantic phenomenon, we can even ask about the extent to which Romantic perceptions of Milton are affected by Romantic findings of the nature of poetry. It is apparent that the official poem and the counterpoem which it either generates or fails to repress can be seen in a variety of relationships. One poem can successfully demolish the other, or be in creative tension with the other, or be locked with the other in destructive conflict. There is perhaps a road here from the Romantics to a wide range of modern understandings.

Shelley responds in more than one way to Milton, and one hopes for an adequate future study of these responses. Among other things, such a study might treat, in relation to each other, Adam's dream as a model for *Alastor, Lycidas* as a model for *Adonais,* and *Paradise Regained* as a model for *Prometheus Unbound.* The creation of Eve in *Paradise Lost* lays down the pattern for an authentic otherness which is organically connected to, yet stands apart from, the self. It is only in relation to this otherness that the self is able to constitute and enlarge its identity. The pattern can stand as a model of social as well as familial relationships. It can even be a model of the relation of the artist to his audience. In *Alastor* the trapped imagination can generate only projections of itself in its compulsive journey to that self-discovery which becomes inevitably self-annihilation. Adam's dream is close to a climax of nightmare. Yet the solitude of the artist may be his creative condition as well as his entrapment. The grimness of the poem is hung upon this paradox.

When even Urania fails to save John Keats, we look back from *Adonais* to Orpheus and forward from the "empty dream" of Calli-

ope to the superior protective force that Milton invokes "In darkness and with dangers compast round." *Adonais* is written in the
presence of *Lycidas,* but there is no "uncouth swain" in *Adonais*
to face the future with that "eager thought" which springs up from
the poem of his self-making. That Urania should fail where Calli-
ope once failed is an indication that no muse can save the poet
from the brute force of the actual and the blind fury of circumstance. It is also and less sentimentally an indication that no muse
can save the poet from himself. Milton's invocations are fraught
with a sense of the presumption of the poetic adventure. The
muse is both instructor and protector against the hubris of seeking
and singing of the ultimate. In *Adonais* it is the naked imagination
which must confront and tear aside the "inmost veil."

Prometheus Unbound, a poem about the regaining of Paradise, would not be what it is without Milton's brief epic. But it is
not an echo of that epic. "Sceptreless, free, uncircumscribed but
man" owes much to Christ's evolving definition of the nature and
primacy of interior kingship. We can even argue that romantic
distinctions between a society that is freely organic and one that is
repressively institutional are finally only transplantations of Milton's discrimination (supported by a long tradition of biblical commentary) of society under the Gospel from society under the Law.
The connection with *Paradise Regained* is then designed to advise
us that we are looking at the secularization of a sacred model—one
in which a liberating relationship with the natural and social order
replaces a liberating dependence on the divine will. *Prometheus
Unbound* is a commentary on the nature of creative humanism,
but it is a commentary whose weight is not fully apparent unless
we relate it to those voices of the past with which it is in discourse. "Discourse" should be the operative word. A poet (as
Yeats's theories of the mask suggest) can regard himself as encountering the past, as confronting it rather than receiving it. But
the styling of the encounter remains within his freedom of maneuver. It is tempting to think that the forms of maneuver must be
eventually classifiable, but this is to minimize the capacity of the
inheritor for invention as well as justice in the endeavor of relat-
edness. Eliot's concept of the "really new" work of art, we must
remember, provides both for continuity and for the force of renewal of the unprecedented.

Bryon is yet another author in whom the Miltonic presence is
rewardingly complex and who deserves the kind of study which it
is hoped these essays will stimulate. He is not one of those who

subscribe to the uniqueness of the Adamic drama. "Mighty pre-
Adamites" have "walked the earth / Of which ours is the wreck"
(*Cain,* 359–60). History restates itself in rhythms of diminution.
Nowhere is Byron's imaginative grasp of this principle more apparent than when Cain and Adah leave Eden, as Adam and Eve left
Paradise. The way ahead is one of desolation rather than dignity,
an angel dispenses reproof where a previous angel provided enlightenment, and an implacable Eve pronounces a curse of unre-
lieved ferocity. The connection with *Paradise Lost* that is invited
provides an enactment of a view of history not less somber than
the one frequently attributed to Milton himself. Byron's backward
look makes it seem almost as if we were looking forward to the
uses of the past in defining the shrinkages of the Waste Land or
the decrescendo into the whimper of the Hollow Men. The suggestion is made because Byron's fascination with the Satanic
proposition that the mind is its own place unduly simplifies our
view of his forms of recourse to Milton. We can wonder, for example, whether the scene of the Destinies in the hall of Arimanes
in *Manfred* reflects a sense of the black comedy of Milton's Sin
and Death well in advance of Joseph Summers' enlightened commentary. Even the Satanic hero who is our most familiar acquaintance with Byronic Miltonics can be seen as alienated from man in
a diminished reflection (befitting Byron's view of history) of his
predecessor's alienation from God. The reflection can be treated
as a completion, and one is left with the uncomfortable possibility
that total alienation may be the price of total selfhood. The Tree of
Knowledge is not that of Life (*Manfred,* 1, 1, 12), and the fruit of
the one may make access to the other impossible. The searching
mind wrenches itself away from those natural and fulfilling relationships which are the declarations of another order of creative-
ness. Byron, it will be apparent, is no straightforward advocate of
the Romantic inversion once taken as the universal response of
the period to Milton. His is yet another way of secularizing the
sacred. The irony (or the appropriateness) is that in pitting itself
against current optimisms, Byron's displacement invokes the same
dominant model.

    Hyperion begins like its pervasive predecessor, in *medias res,*
in the hell of "lost happiness" (*PL* I, 55) and with a council of the
dispossessed. The obvious difference is that the expulsion of Satan preserved the status quo; that of the Titans superseded the
order for which the Titans stood. Progress was once found in the
holding down of rebellion, the limitation of the force of destruc-

tiveness. It is now to be found in the acceptance of revolution. The Miltonic apparatus richly invoked, but surrounding a different situation, helps to advise us of the pain of the way forward as the Atonement once advised us of the cost of the way back. We are made to confront from the beginning the poem's "weight of woe," its immensity of loss, and to move through it to a realization of the expense as well as the necessity of the proposition that "first in beauty should be first in might."

Lycidas is a poem about the validity of poetry. Eliot's oeuvre is a macro-poem about the possibility of language. In drawing a line through these points we can see how the destruction of Paradise in the eleventh book of *Paradise Lost* points not only to the paradise within as the climax of Milton's epic, but to the poem of the future as the heroic poem of consciousness. Wordsworth's remarkable achievement in this genre—a poem of the mind in which the formed mind presides over the story of its formation—will lead to a poem which situates the reader within the journeying mind itself, within the self-making endeavor of the advancing consciousness. The poet's dialogue with Moneta in *The Fall of Hyperion* is, as Douglas Bush suggests, a crucial stage in the evolution of this poem of self-making for which the inclusive and not very distant models are *Paradise Regained* and *Samson Agonistes* as well as *Lycidas*. One should not omit *Areopagitica,* with its images of sifting and discerning, of cumulative gathering and building. These models clearly point the way forward in that they tell us of structure discovered through process. The Romantic taking-up of these models (and of the views of organic form they anticipate) may be a more important admission of the Miltonic presence than those stylistic acknowledgments in which Romantic poetry is not lacking.

Verbal remembrance is not the only or even the most important ingredient of the Miltonic presence, but for many critics verbal remembrance remains the index of influence. Such remembrances are all too often treated as local rather than contextual, as emulation diminishing into mimicry. The straitjacket of the grand style is a natural petrification when style is all that allusion seeks to evoke. The essays in this volume should rescue us from these simplifications, showing how the poetry of allusive reference to Milton involves the commentary of one poem on another as part of the advancement of a heritage. Indeed it could be said that the poetry of allusion after Milton profits from the tactics of allusion that Milton himself developed, and that the presence of Milton is nowhere stronger than in making more creative our uses of the past. In a school which it was desirable to establish, Eliot is surely among the more distinguished pupils.

The diversities of presence so far considered include the stylistic and the verbal, the structural and the mythopoeic, the secularization of the sacred, the poem as a model of reality, and the poem as a mimesis of the self-achieving consciousness. Other manifestations can be added to what is by now a sufficiently formidable list. The contributors to this volume trace Milton's presence in many forms; but whatever the form, they find it liberating rather than restrictive. Anxiety is not characteristically the guiding force in the relationship, and reading is involved as often as misreading. This is not to deny the existence of evasion, of "revisionary poetics," and even of inversion as historic responses to Milton's accomplishment. Indeed, an interesting complication of "displacement" might begin with an inversion that the Romantics progressively came to take for granted and then proceed to a revision of the inversion thus accepted. Furthermore, as my essay on Eliot suggests, misprision or studious circumvention may well be a natural mode of relationship with the past until the order-seeking consciousness has advanced to a point where a more direct confrontation is possible. But Milton's frames of discourse and imagining remain of importance to other writers who, even after they have been educated into devising a frame of their own, maintain its relationship with the frames that Milton established. The evolving dialogue with the past thus created is a necessary part of the continuity of poetry. The deeper poetry finds and declares itself as a persisting metaphysical language, a language kept in being by a "concern with speech." Milton's work provides us with some of the elements in the grammar of comprehension that articulates that language.

B. RAJAN

MILTON STUDIES

XI

DRYDEN'S ADMIRED ACQUAINTANCE, MR. MILTON

Earl Miner

> Mr. Milton, whom we all admire with such justice.
> —John Dryden, 1693

THE EXACT nature of the relationship between Dryden and Milton will never be known in detail, and in spite of a number of studies about Milton's relations with his younger contemporaries, the general state of critical opinion is remarkably selective of what knowledge we do have.[1] The stubborn plainness of the facts we possess seems to have freed some critics to enjoy inference and conjecture. The most we can hope for is that conjecture be distinguished from fact, that dates be attended to, and that the absence of evidence not be taken as evidence. As an example of the last consideration, even a very able critic of the personal emotions of Dryden and of Pope as sons of Milton (and of Dryden) presumes a Freudian uneasiness with the father.[2] Milton and Dryden had their vanities and differing ambitions, but there is no evidence at all to suggest that Dryden felt anxiety toward a poetic father. In fact, any impartial observer of literary tyros must be surprised by the good relations between these two poets, and in particular by Dryden's public kindness to the blind poet.

Dryden's response is not prima facie inevitable. Milton was temperamentally haughty, Dryden diffident. They were widely divided on the political and religious issues of the time. More than all that—although implied by it—they were contemporaries. This fact distinguishes Dryden from any other poet of importance whose poetry was influenced in a major degree by Milton. Dryden (1631–1700) was only in his teens when Milton's *Poems* of 1645 was published, whereas Milton (1608–1674) was already thirty-seven. But by the time Milton published his next volume of poetry, the ten-book version of *Paradise Lost* (1667), Dryden was the best-known dramatist of the time and recently distinguished for publication of a narrative poem of some length, *Annus Mirabilis*. Cowley, Dave-

3

nant, William Chamberlayne, Butler, and Dryden had all preceded Milton as published narrative poets. Farfetched notions about Milton as "the last Elizabethan" (that queen had died unpopular five years before Milton was born) suggest more about the people holding them than about Milton. The Milton who matters to world literature is—like Butler, Marvell, and Dryden—a poet whose world view took its distinctive character during the Interregnum and the early Restoration. When all is said, however, the established facts remain few. As poets, Milton and Dryden are contemporaries. Both belong to that last phase of the Renaissance (or first phase after the Renaissance) when the genres were once again reordered in favor of narrative and drama rather than the lyric. The distinctive character of both men's poetry is its public mode and personal commitment. Rudely put, John Milton and John Dryden—products of similar education and two revolutions in the state—are Restoration poets.

I. Acquaintance and Encounter

The clearest, best-documented acknowledgment of relations between the two poets appears to be Dryden's in the fourth edition of *Paradise Lost*. This appeared in 1688, after Milton had been dead nearly a decade and a half, but it tells us in retrospect something of the relationship between them. Among the more than five hundred subscribers to this first illustrated edition was Dryden, who also supplied the publisher with one of his two epigrams:

> Three *Poets*, in three distant *Ages* born,
> *Greece, Italy,* and *England* did adorn.
> The *First* in loftiness of thought surpass'd;
> The *Next* in Majesty; in both the *Last*.
> The force of *Nature* cou'd no farther goe:
> To make a *Third* she joynd the former two.

Neither Dryden nor Milton had a special genius for short poems, but these lines testify to Dryden's knowledge of Milton's tastes and of his so-called minor poems as well as of *Paradise Lost*. For among the complimentary poems that Milton eagerly used to boost his *Poems,* there is a distich by one Selvaggi, whom he had met at Rome:

> Graecia Maeonidem, jactet sibi Roma Maronem,
> Anglia Miltonum jactat utrique parem.

Dryden knew that Milton would have been pleased by a compliment originating with an Italian, and that his pride would have been soothed at being termed equal to Homer and Virgil. Such compliments were seldom taken seriously in the seventeenth century—except perhaps by the recipients—but Dryden's version joined to *Paradise Lost* makes sense, whereas Selvaggi's is founded on no sounder basis than Mediterranean compliment.

We cannot be certain when Dryden read what he termed Milton's juvenilia. It seems most unlikely that he did so before 1673, when the 1645 *Poems* had a second edition adding some poems and prose and omitting a few poems that might offend the new regime. Selvaggi's distich is there, and we shall later see that Dryden recalled *Lycidas* and perhaps *Comus*. Sometime between 1673 and 1688 Dryden had a copy of Milton's *Poems* before him, and for reasons that will emerge, I think the year could not have been before that of second publication.

What of Milton? Apart from giving the world his three principal poems between 1667 and 1671, he held to a public silence as marked as his earlier boldness in prose. One would give a good deal to read Milton on himself after 1660. We do have a little evidence to speculate over. The first edition of *Paradise Lost* sold reasonably well, but the bookseller naturally tried to promote sales and so in 1668 brought out the ten-book version augmented. Simmons prefixed an advertisement, *"The Printer to the Reader"*:

Courteous Reader, There was no Argument at first intended to the Book, but for the satisfaction of many that have desired it, I have procur'd it, and withall a reason of that which stumbled many others, why the Poem Rimes not.

Milton must have thought understandable a desire for arguments to the books of so long a poem. But his note on "The Verse" shows that he bristled over the idea that narratives should rhyme: "Not without cause therefore some both *Italian* and *Spanish* Poets of prime note have rejected Rime both in longer and shorter Works, as have also long since our best *English* Tragedies." Milton is remarkably sparing of examples, and simply because Dryden was eminently living and rhyming at that hour, some have thought Milton to be attacking his wayward contemporary. Actually, Milton is defending himself. Among those poets of prime note who used rhyme in narrative poems, we must include Dante, Tasso, and Ariosto; Camões; Spenser, Marlowe, Shakespeare, and their contemporaries; and Milton's seventeenth-century precursors, including Butler and Dryden. No wonder Milton's blank verse stumbled many readers.

Protestant and neoclassicist to the end, Milton thought he was reforming by returning to the true prosody of lofty verse. He follows Homer and Virgil rather than that "Invention of a barbarous Age," rhyme. He will not be "carried away by Custom" like "some famous modern poets." How wide all this is of the mark! The blank verse of *Paradise Lost* is its own justification. Clearly Milton's old spirit of controversy had been aroused. By whom? Or, considered another way, who are those "famous modern Poets" who endured the vexation of rhyme? I have named nine or more, but some critics have suggested Dryden. This would mean that someone had read *Annus Mirabilis* to Milton, a not impossible thing. But the evident fact is that the printer, Simmons, had put Milton on the defensive by the implicit judgment that no great narrative poem had been written in unrhymed verse for centuries.

The closest student of the relations between Milton and Dryden has argued that "to understand fully Milton's preface on rhyme to *Paradise Lost*, . . . we must relate it to the contemporary extended debate between Dryden and Sir Robert Howard."[3] Quite possibly. The debate rattled through prefaces and was the subject of studied argument in *An Essay of Dramatic Poesy*. Milton's remarks say nothing of French poets, it will be recalled, although during 1664 and 1665 Sorbière had deprecated, and Sprat justified, English drama for its avoidance of rhyme.[4] Can we conclude of Milton's paragraph that "almost every phrase is the distillation of lengthy matter in Dryden and Howard"?[5] I remain doubtful. The arguments had long been familiar, and one might as easily credit as their origin Jonson's "Fit of Rime Against Rime."

If Milton was glancing at Dryden, it was at Dryden in the company of almost all other "modern" narrative poets, or at Dryden as the principal theoretical exponent of rhyme in heroic plays and tragedies. The latter possibility is likelier in terms of Dryden's special role, but I do not find it easy to believe that Milton frequented the theater to hear *The Indian Emperor* or *Secret-Love*. It is just conceivable that someone read to Milton from the quartos of those plays and, more likely, the text of *An Essay of Dramatic Poesy* or *Annus Mirabilis*. My guess is that if Milton did have Dryden in mind as a principal example of those who rhyme, it was a version of Dryden gained secondhand from those who had read his verse, plays, and criticism. It is therefore possible but unprovable that Milton was taking aim at Dryden. Those who believe as much must also accept two other things: that Milton publicly referred to Dryden before Dryden to him; and that Milton's attention to his younger contemporary involved attacking Dryden's early art in narrative and dramatic verse.

It is a separate question whether Dryden took Milton's paragraph as an attack. Once again the answer is that we lack proof, but some things may be observed. Neither Dryden nor for that matter Howard referred to Milton's arguments at this time. Dryden went on writing rhymed poetry for the rest of his life. Dryden's famous avowal that he would desert his long-loved mistress rhyme was made in the Prologue to *Aureng-Zebe* (1676). But we must not make too much of that.[6] After all, most of *The Rival Ladies* (1664) had been in blank verse, which he continued to use in combination with rhyme in the theater, until he turned once again to blank verse as his verse medium for elevated drama. We may presume that if Dryden read Milton's stricture, he was unmoved. Surely he thought that *Paradise Lost* was a great narrative poem eccentric in its prosody.

The attempt to set Milton and Dryden to quarreling reveals a good deal about the attempters, but little about the poets. What evidence we have does not show that they knew each other personally before 1667 or 1669, when Milton had seven or five years to live. They moved, as it were, in directions that would sometimes cross on the same current of literary as well as political events. Such as it is, the positive evidence—like the absence of evidence—suggests that relations between the two poets were cordial and began within a couple of years of the publication of *Paradise Lost*, but not before.

The most reliable testimony from a contemporary of the two poets comes from the irresistible but unscientific Aubrey. His jottings on the blind poet contain much derived from Milton's nephew, Edward Phillips, and from Milton's brother Christopher. Aubrey may well have had some things firsthand or from Marvell, but he certainly got some from Dryden. Milton, we learn, was a

temperate man, rarely dranke between meales. Extreme pleasant in his conversation, and at dinner, supper, etc; but Satyricall. (He pronounced the letter R (*littera canina*) very hard—a certaine signe of a Satyricall Witt—*from John Dreyden*.)[7]

Dryden's testimony about Milton's temperate habits causes no surprise, but it is a delight to have his attestation on Milton's "pleasant" conversations at mealtime. As for Milton's being "Satyricall," some may wonder what the poet of *Mac Flecknoe* could possibly have meant about the poet of *Paradise Lost*. Dryden's first satire was written, however, about four years after Milton's death. In the absence of contrary evidence, the fair assumption seems to be that Milton and Dryden enjoyed each other's company, however frequent or infrequent it was.

The most striking anecdote concerning Dryden's attitude toward Milton is well attested to but not wholly proved. If true, it would account completely for Dryden's visiting Milton and appreciating his conversation. In his *Explanatory Notes and Remarks on Milton's Paradise Lost* (1734), Jonathan Richardson passed on a story from Sir Fleetwood Sheppard, who knew Dorset and Dryden. Dorset, so the account goes, happened on *Paradise Lost* at a bookseller's in 1669 and was taken by some passages that caught his attention. When he purchased a copy,

the bookseller begged him to speak in its favour if he liked it, for they lay on his hands as waste paper—Jesus! [Actually, the first edition was exhausted in 1669.] Sheppard was present. My Lord took it home, read it, and sent it to Dryden, who in a short time returned it: "This man," says Dryden, "cuts us all out, and the ancients too."[8]

Nothing here except the error about sales is impossible, and the transmission has a firmer line than is characteristic of most else that has come down to us about relations between the two poets. In a sense, the imputed comment is morally if not factually true, because Dryden very soon treated *Paradise Lost* and *Paradise Regained* as classics to be alluded to and otherwise used as norms of value, like poems by Virgil, Ovid, and Horace. It is very difficult indeed to think of another English poet who has regarded a contemporary as a classic. Richardson's report has some confirmation from Aubrey, whose jottings on Milton mention how foreigners sought him out during the Protectorate. Aubrey then speaks of a later time:

His familiar learned Acquaintance were Mr Andrew Marvell, Mr [Robert] Skinner, Dr [Nathan] Pagett, M.D.

John Dreyden, Esq, Poet Laureate, who very much admires him, went to him to have leave to putt his *Paradise Lost* into a Drame in Rhyme. Mr Milton received him civilly, and told him *he would give him leave to tagge his Verses.*[9]

There is reason to think that Dryden wrote his so-called opera, *The State of Innocence,* for the marriage of James to Mary of Este and Modena in November 1673.[10] For whatever reason, the play was not performed, although Dryden's later remarks imply that he had discovered, as had Milton before him, that the Fall of Man was no subject for "a Drame." Manuscripts of Dryden's version, some of which survive, were in circulation, however, and in 1677 Dryden at last published it to get a correct text abroad. Dryden's dramatic version certainly was misguided, but it cannot be seen to have occasioned any difference between him and Milton. The "opera" caps some four years of Dryden's acquaintance with Milton's epic and with the poet himself.

Such events—proven, probable, or merely possible—bring us to 1674. Before Milton died on November 8, *Paradise Lost* appeared in its twelve-book second edition, the version familiar ever since. Advertised in July, the new edition appeared (five years after Dryden's first reading?) with an effusively encomiastic poem by Dr. Samuel Borrow, along with a curious poem by Marvell, "On Paradise Lost." His first sixteen lines express apprehension that Milton would "ruine . . . sacred Truths" (7–8). If Milton were to succeed, "some less skilful hand / . . . Might hence presume the whole Creations day / To change in Scenes, and show it in a Play" (18, 21–22). We lack evidence to show that Marvell had read *The State of Innocence* in manuscript. In fact "the whole Creations day" is as odd a description of Dryden's action as of Milton's. But it does seem that Marvell had heard of Dryden's project: Who else planned to "show it in a Play"? I do not think it has been observed that it is Marvell, in this poem, who introduces a querulous note that had been absent in the known relations between Milton and Dryden. Nor has it been remarked that, by some strange coincidence, *The State of Innocence* was published with a commendatory poem by Nathaniel Lee that presciently urges Dryden toward what was to be *Absalom and Achitophel*, or that it contains an apparent reference to Marvell:

> On then, O mightiest of the inspired men!
> Monarch of verse! new themes employ thy pen.
> The troubles of majestic Charles set down;
> Not David vanquished more to reach a crown.
> Praise him as Cowley did that Hebrew king:
> Thy theme's as great; do thou as greatly sing.
> Then thou may'st boldly to his favour rise,
> Look down, and the base serpent's hiss despise;
> From thund'ring envy safe in laurel sit,
> While clam'rous critics their vile heads submit,
> Condemn'd for treason at the bar of wit.[11]

It can only be assumed that Lee had the political and critical Marvell principally in mind in a poem that commends Dryden in an encomium parallel to Marvell's on Milton. Once again, the quarrel picked was not of Dryden's making or Milton's. And by then the gout-stricken Milton was dead.

II. MILTON IN DRYDEN'S POETRY

At the death of Milton, Dryden was preeminent in drama but not the greatest living nondramatic poet in England. That title must be given to Marvell or Butler. In the quarter of a century more that Dryden was to live, however, he displaced all rivals, developing in ways that could not have been foretold. Milton has some place in his development, as we can discover from allusions in his poetry, remarks in his prose, and aims expressed for poetry. Editors and critics alert to echoes have detailed many of his allusions to Milton, and a selection of these can show us how Milton became a presence in Dryden's poetry.

The State of Innocence was fundamentally misguided and often seems strained or flat. But there are good things also:

> all the sad variety of hell [Lucifer]
> (Alas, that we must measure time by woe) [Lucifer]
> Knowledge and innocence are perfect joy [Raphael]
> If this be dreaming, let me never wake [Adam]

All this is distinctly Drydenian. In one particular, however, it may be asked—as it has been—whether Dryden was not more Miltonic than Milton.[12] In Book III of *Paradise Lost,* Milton had concerned himself with justifying free will in a providential order governed by a prescient and omnipotent God. This problem becomes more prominent in Dryden's version, exercising Satan in his debate with Gabriel and Ithuriel in Act III, and monopolizing the discussion between Adam and Raphael in Act IV. Similarly, late in his life Dryden was to be more Chaucerian than Chaucer in expanding on Chaucer's concern with these matters for his *Cock and the Fox* (The Nun's Priest's Tale).

Most readers of Dryden today are more interested in what lies between *The State of Innocence* and the poems in *Fables. Mac Flecknoe* very much involves what Lee termed the "Monarch of Verse," although in the debased versions of Flecknoe and Mac Flecknoe/Shadwell. As I have said in *Dryden's Poetry,* the poem is founded on a mock-play of a coronation in its action, and on monarchy, poetry or art, and religion in its metaphorical strands. The most obvious allusion to Milton involves all these strains: "The hoary Prince in Majesty appear'd, / High on a Throne of his own Labours rear'd" (106–07). The "Labours" refer to Flecknoe's works, published at his own expense. The clear Miltonic echo also places that monarch of nonsense:

> High on a Throne of Royal State, which far
> Outshon the wealth of *Ormus* and of *Ind*,
> Or where the gorgeous East with richest hand
> Showrs on her Kings *Barbaric* Pearl and Gold,
> Satan exalted sat.

So Milton (*PL* II, 1–5). The central point of this echo is that referred to before: within eleven years of the epic's publication, and perhaps within nine of Dryden's reading *Paradise Lost*, he assumes that it is a sufficiently great, shared, and public achievement to be deemed a classic—and this by a contemporary of the alluding poet. As a classic or norm, that poem can be used by the new poet and his readers to "place" the shoddy version offered by Flecknoe. Dryden was sufficiently assured on this score to give a positive version of the motif some sixteen years later in his poem to Congreve:

> Yet this I Prophecy; Thou shalt be seen,
> (Tho' with some short Parenthesis between:)
> High on the Throne of Wit.   (51–53)

The special Miltonic-Drydenian version of the old *topos* was well enough established for Pope to echo Dryden echoing Milton at the beginning of the second book of *The Dunciad*.

A less familiar example from *Mac Flecknoe* will show how fully Milton's coloring enters the fabric of the poem. The narrator introduces Flecknoe as he is about to enter into his second harangue:

> The *Syre* then shook the honours of his head,
> And from his brows damps of oblivion shed
> Full on the filial dullness: long he stood,
> Repelling from his Breast the raging God;
> At length burst out in this prophetick mood.   (134–38)

Here is a tissue of allusion. There are three to the *Aeneid:* the behavior of Jupiter in X, 113–15; the frenzy of the Sibyl in VI, 46–51; and Helenus' prophecy when possessed by the god in III, 369 ff. Dryden's allusion to Milton provides his evaluation of the Virgilian allusions. Milton's passage appears in *Paradise Lost:*

> He said, and on his Son with Rayes direct
> Shon full, he all his Father full expresst
> Ineffably into his face receiv'd.   (VI, 719–21)

The Flecknovian dullness and gloom had once been full and radi-
ant. In such fashion, although Virgil probably amounts to more in
Mac Flecknoe, Milton proves decisive by virtue of Dryden's use of
him as a poetic and religious norm.

　　Absalom and Achitophel uses Milton equally decisively and
more at large. As is widely known, there are a number of echoes of
Paradise Lost and even an unmistakable imitation: "Him Stagger-
ing so when Hells dire Agent found" (373). But it is to *Paradise
Regained* that the action of Dryden's poem is most indebted.
Achitophel's attempt to seduce Absalom into action against David
draws upon Satan's temptation of the kingdoms in Milton's brief
epic. A central feature of the temptation anticipates Barbara K.
Lewalski's discussion of Satan's use of religious typology to seduce the Son.[13] She shows that Satan seeks to get the Son to
identify himself with an inferior type or to relate himself to an
earlier type in some improper way. Dryden recognized what has
been rediscovered only so recently, having his tempter, Achitophel, use typology to becloud the mind of Absalom:

> Auspicious Prince! at whose Nativity
> Some Royal Planet rul'd the Southern sky
> . . . .
> Their second *Moses*,
> . . . .
> Thee, *Saviour*, Thee, the Nations Vows confess. 　　(230–40)

Achitophel works not on the Son of God to get him to belittle his
exalted role, but on Absalom to get him to sin through aspiring
pride in falsely thinking of himself as our "Saviour." This very
complex use of Milton shows how well Dryden understood his
senior, that classic born a mere twenty-three years before him.

　　Dryden's ease in adapting Milton appears in a passage echoing *Paradise Lost* (I, 500–02) where the narrator reprehends—or
so many have thought—profligate courtiers around Charles II:

> And when Night
> Darkens the Streets, then wander forth the Sons
> Of *Belial*, flown with insolence and wine.

Dryden's echo is sounded in his character of Shimei, or Slingsby
Bethel, who had the distinction of plotting against both Cromwell
and Charles:

> During his Office, Treason was no Crime;
> The Sons of *Belial* had a glorious Time. 　　(597–98)

This allusion pays Milton another compliment of understanding his art. As we all know, Milton again and again uses pagan material for its evocative power only to dismiss it in advance by the proviso, "to compare great things to small," or in retrospect with a "thus they relate erring." Dryden makes the Sons of Belial into something not fully intended by Milton—into rebels and, more than that, into rebels against a Stuart king. It is quite possible that Dryden's phrase also means "the sons of Balliol," since that college was a center of intrigue against Charles when Parliament sat in Oxford toward the close of the Exclusion Crisis. In any event, here is triumphant tagging of Milton's poem by effecting a radical transformation.

Thenceforth such free revisionism marks Dryden's use of Milton. Among the many examples that might be given, we may consider portions of the long passage on the Catholic Church in the second part of *The Hind and the Panther:*

> So when of old th' Almighty father sate
> In Council, to redeem our ruin'd state,
> Millions of millions at a distance round,
> Silent the sacred Consistory crown'd,
> To hear what mercy mixt with justice cou'd propound;
> All prompt with eager pity, to fulfill
> The full extent of their Creatour's will:
> But when the stern conditions were declar'd,
> A mournfull whisper through the host was heard,
> And the whole hierarchy with heads hung down
> Submissively declin'd the pondrous proffer'd crown.
> Then, not till then, th' eternal Son from high
> Rose in the strength of all the Deity;
> Stood forth t' accept the terms, and underwent
> A weight which all the frame of heav'n had bent,
> Nor he Himself cou'd bear, but as omnipotent.
> Now, to remove the least remaining doubt,
> That ev'n the blear-ey'd sects may find her out,
> Behold what heav'nly rays adorn her brows,
> What from his Wardrobe her belov'd allows
> To deck the wedding-day of his unspotted spouse.
> Behold what marks of majesty she brings;
> Richer than ancient heirs of Eastern kings:
> Her right hand holds the sceptre and the keys,
> To shew whom she commands, and who obeys:
> With these to bind, or set the sinner free,
> With that t' assert spiritual Royalty.
> . . . .

Still when the Gyant-brood invades her throne
She stoops from heav'n, and meets 'em half way down,
And with paternal thunder vindicates her crown.

(499–525, 535–37)

Long as it is, the quotation offers a brilliant condensation and adaptation of one of the crucial moments in *Paradise Lost* and, if truth be said, has appealed to readers more than has its original. In the third book of Milton's poem (56–343, for Dryden especially 203–65), God speaks of his providential plan, of man's sin, and of the need for satisfaction of divine justice. The Son offers himself as sacrifice. Dryden recalls the central Christian and Miltonic point. Whatever Pope said about Milton's God speaking like a school divine, Dryden's passage is, in Sir Walter Scott's words, "extremely beautiful." Dryden achieves his effect by avoiding introduction of God as a character—an introduction that even Milton could not successfully effect—stressing instead Jesus Christ and his Church. It is that (Roman Catholic) Church who plays the role of defeating the opposition in the gigantomachy (for example, see *Metamorphoses*, I, 151–55; *Georgics*, I, 28–83), and she does so by taking on the role of Milton's Son in his Father's chariot defeating the rebel angels.[14] As a Christian, Dryden obviously retains the centrality of Christ, even while giving a Catholic emphasis to the Church. He continues, then, to draw on Milton as a classic representing essential values, yet he does so after the Miltonic manner, finely replacing or wholly revising what he has respectfully borrowed.

In all this there is no Romantic angst over a great predecessor. *The State of Innocence* reveals awe misapplied, but as Dryden's genius matures, he simply takes on Milton's habit of appropriating to radically different ends what he borrows. He differs from Milton only in not dismissing his source with some "Satyricall" phrase.

Many more examples might be given of Dryden's use of Milton's heroic poetry. Indeed, no one could expect him to write sonnets, but that is not to say that he was unaware of Milton's early verse. The question of what he might use from those poems could be fairly answered from his use of Donne's poems on the death of Elizabeth Drury for his own *Eleonora* (1692). In the well-known analysis of *The Anniversaries* into sections, Louis L. Martz has shown that each of the two poems alternates passages such as meditations and eulogies that vary markedly in tone.[15] Dryden unerringly recalls the eulogistic passages, forgetting the alarmed complaints over this sorry world.

Given such a habit of mind, Dryden should not surprise us by recalling *Lycidas* to praise the dead composer Henry Purcell, or by altering what he takes to suit his own conception of human dignity and the Christian dispensation. Christian poets writing memorial poems encounter problems in creating a sense of real grief and in affording it a place in a providential scheme. Both such Christian concerns and his own faith in the capacities of gifted individuals lead Dryden to omit grief from any of his memorials in which there is a Christian emphasis. "To the Memory of Mr. Oldham" is perhaps the sole exception in conveying grief, and significantly all its allusions are classical, pagan. Purcell was probably as well known to Dryden as was Oldham, but he was not someone for whom the now old poet had paternal hopes, and his death did not come before truly great achievement. For such reasons, when Dryden wrote his "Ode on the Death of Mr. Henry Purcell" (1696), he surrounded the man so inevitably termed Orpheus Britannicus with glory rather than with gloom. As Orpheus, Purcell had demonstrated immortal achievement. As a *British* Orpheus, he was a Christian.

Milton certainly possessed an interest in music at least equal to Dryden's, and an interest in the figure of Orpheus as a representative of the artist and his fate. This is shown by a familiar passage in *Lycidas* that seeks to assign blame and grieves over loss:

> Where were ye Nymphs when the remorseless deep
> Clos'd o're the head of your lov'd *Lycidas?*
> · · · · · · · ·
> Ay me, I fondly dream!
> Had ye bin there—for what could that have don?
> What could the Muse her self that *Orpheus* bore,
> The Muse her self for her inchanting son
> Whom Universal nature did lament,
> When by the rout that made the hideous roar,
> His goary visage down the stream was sent,
> Down the swift *Hebrus* to the *Lesbian* shore.   (50–51, 56–63)

Dryden recalls that the old Orpheus had sought his wife in Hades before losing her on his return and before suffering the fate to which Milton refers. Dryden posits that pagan Orpheus as a type of "our *Orpheus*," the Christian fulfillment, Purcell:

> We beg not Hell, our *Orpheus* to restore,
> Had He been there,
> Their Sovereigns fear
> Had sent Him back before.

> The pow'r of Harmony too well they know,
> He long e'er this had Tun'd their jarring Sphere
>   And left no Hell below.   (16–22)

The contrast between Milton's pagan Orpheus and Dryden's
Christian one emerges most forcibly in the clearest echo of *Lycidas*. Milton addresses the Nymphs—"Had ye been there"—but
what could they have done, any more than the Muse could do
anything for Orpheus? To Dryden, it is all a very strong subjunc-
tive concerning Purcell: "Had he been there"—he would have
tuned hell away with his harmony. But in fact "our *Orpheus*" has
gone to heaven.

At the end of *Lycidas*, Milton moves with apparent sudden-
ness and evident magnificence to his vision of Edward King in
heaven:

> There entertain him all the Saints above,
> In solemn troops, and sweet Societies
> That sing, and singing in their glory move,
> And wipe the tears for ever from his eyes.   (178–81)

Dryden had been presuming as much of Purcell all along. With
such a presumption, he can dwell on the more metaphysical notion (compare Donne's vision of the soul's progress in the second
Anniversary) of Purcell's translation to heaven and on a very different relation to singing angels:

> The Heav'nly Quire, who heard his Notes from high,
> Let down the Scale of Musick from the Sky:
>   They handed him along,
> And all the way He taught, and all the way they Sung.   (23–26)

The scale of music was depicted as a ladderlike figure designating
harmonic intervals, and sometimes the Ptolemaic spheres and of
course their notes.[16] From this ode we can see how Dryden recalled Milton's concern with death, loss, and glorification in a poem
written fifty-eight years earlier. And we can see how he transformed that concern into a paean on human worth, on the centrality
of art to life, and on the providential scheme. Milton matters in the
recollection. He matters, that is, as Dryden finds him to matter in
the new world that he discovered his poetry must treat.

III. MILTON IN DRYDEN'S LITERARY SPHERE

From about 1669 to Milton's death in 1674, Dryden could
only conceive of him as a great contemporary and a great classic as

well. The absence of echoes or favorable references by Dryden to Marvell after his poems were published in 1681 shows that the M.P. for Hull did not matter in Dryden's conception of a new era of literature. If Marvell was irrelevant, Samuel Butler was different: a narrative, learned, and satiric poet—who pronounced his *r* very hard? The Earl of Rochester intruded himself on Dryden, who admired that brilliant figure for a time before they drew apart in mutual distrust. Rochester resented Dryden's great plans for a new literature and captaincy in it. Dryden disliked Rochester's profligacy and aristocratic arrogance. In all this, these two other principal Restoration poets obviously do not play the role in Dryden's imagination that Milton does. And if Dryden had his brushes with Rochester, that only testifies the more eloquently to his admiration for Milton.

This is not to say that Dryden's references to Milton are uniformly laudatory. His comments on Milton in his critical writings do not conflict with his poetic treatments of Milton, but they do offer us a somewhat different view. To *The State of Innocence* (1677) Dryden prefixed "The Author's Apology for Heroic Poetry and Poetic License." The heroic here means the heroic play as much as epic, but in the essay we discover some technical matters of a more general kind. Renaissance critics worried in particular about language. Milton and Dryden obviously diverged on the proper language of poetry. Like Spenser, Milton created a language of art that made no pretense to representing what Jonson termed "deeds and language such as men do use." Like Jonson and Donne, Dryden sought to create more of a natural langauge seemingly close to speech and "the other harmony of prose." Of course Milton knew his mother tongue and Dryden the "terms of art." So it is that in his apology Dryden defends "the flights of heroic poetry" above common speech, defending Homer, Virgil, Tasso, and "Milton's *Paradise*."[17] As part of a general case for elevated poetry, he also defends Homer and Virgil for "interesting their gods in the wars of Troy and Italy," arguing that Horace himself would not "have taxed Milton, as our false critics have presumed to do, for his choice of a supernatural argument."[18] The only printed comments on Milton by that time were the poems by Barrows and Marvell. Indeed it seems certain that Dryden felt apprehensive over what Thomas Rymer had on his mind when, at the close of his *Tragedies of the Last Age* published the next year (1678), he threatened some future attack on Milton.

Years later, in the long and rambling "Discourse" introducing

his translation of the *Satires* of Juvenal and Persius, Dryden pays
particular attention to Milton:

As for Mr Milton, whom we all admire with so much justice, his subject
[in *Paradise Lost*] is not that of a heroic poem, properly so called. His
design is the losing of our happiness; his event [outcome] is not prosper-
ous, like that of all other epic works; his heavenly machines are many,
and his human persons are but two. But I will not take Mr Rymer's work
out of his hands. He has promised the world a critique on that author;
wherein, tho' he will not allow his poem for heroic, I hope he will grant
that his thoughts are elevated, his words sounding, and that no man has so
happily copied the manner of Homer; or so copiously translated his Grecisms, and the Latin elegancies of Virgil.[19]

To one who has studied Dryden's indirections for some years,
Dryden is entering a few criticisms of Milton precisely to forestall
"Rymer's work." Dryden goes on to say that Milton may run "into
a flat of thought" and that the blank verse may be excused, if not
justified, because it rather than rhyme was his congenial medium,
as Milton's "juvenilia" show. Fortunately, Milton criticism has not
yet fallen into the bardolatry of Shakespeare criticism, so that
those of us who think *Paradise Lost* the greatest poem in the
language can consider with Dryden that any human production
will have limitations. But the important fact is that Rymer's long-
promised attack never appeared. I believe that by such a mixture
of small criticisms and (yet again) by junction of Milton with
Homer and Virgil, Dryden forestalled the promised attack by the
learned but acerbic and hidebound Rymer.

Later in the "Discourse," Dryden again considers the language of elevated poetry. Waller and Denham are not quite adequate. Neither is Cowley, whom he termed "the darling of my
youth" and whom (according to report) Milton thought next greatest after Shakespeare and Spenser:

Then I consulted a greater genius [than Cowley] . . . , I mean Milton. But
as he endeavours everywhere to express Homer, whose age had not arrived to that fineness, I found in him a true sublimity, lofty thoughts,
which were clothed with admirable Grecisms, and ancient words. . . . But
I found not there neither that for which I looked. At last I had recourse to
his master Spenser, . . . and there I met with that which I had been looking for so long in vain. Spenser had studied Virgil to as much advantage
as Milton had done Homer; and amongst the rest of his excellencies had
copied that.[20]

The idea of Virgilian Spenser lies beyond my powers to explicate
in any meaningful, detailed way. But Dryden's habit of drawing

parallels clearly led him at this juncture to consider Milton the English Homer and Spenser the English Virgil. Since Dryden was about to translate Virgil, his usual enthusiasm for his present object of attention led him to extol the two Virgils. Milton gets his credits, but the idea that a Virgil came before a Homer in English poetry is more suggestive critically than historically.

Dryden finally settled his view of English literary history in his Preface to *Fables*. He is talking of the adequacy of translations of Ovid:

He who has arrived the nearest to it, is the ingenious and learned Sandys, the best versifier of the former age; if I may properly call it by that name, which was the former part of this concluding century. For Spenser and Fairfax both flourished in the reign of Queen Elizabeth; great masters in our language, and who saw much farther into the beauties of our numbers than those who immediately followed them. Milton was the poetical son of Spenser, and Mr Waller of Fairfax; for we have our lineal descents and clans as well as other families: Spenser more than once insinuates that the soul of Chaucer was transfused into his body; and that he was begotten by him two hundred years after his decease. Milton has acknowledged to me that Spenser was his original; and many besides myself have heard our famous Waller own that he derived the harmony of his numbers from *Godfrey of Bulloign*, which was turned into English by Mr Fairfax.[21]

Much in this may be fanciful. But apart from all else, there are two conceptions of literary history bequeathed us by Dryden. One is the conception of an age or a literary era, which he introduced into literary thought in England.[22] If the idea of an age is a historical fiction, we have not yet found means to do without it in literary or other kinds of history. Dryden's other concept is of "lineal descents" or "clans"—lines of influence or major authorial traditions within literature. For this he postulates two lines of poetry from earlier times to his own age. There is the line of refined poetry: Fairfax to Waller—and Denham? And there is the line of genius: Chaucer to Spenser to Milton—and no doubt also to Dryden himself. If there were a doubt, the poem following the Preface (to the Duchess of Ormonde) should dispel it. Again we find, in the opening lines, Homer, Virgil, Chaucer, and—since he is redoing Chaucer—none other than Dryden himself. The claim is wholly implicit to be sure, but Chaucer and Dryden each has his Emily.

Dryden's claims, like all such claims, rested on hope. He had a lifelong obsession with the epic and its subgeneric quality, the heroic.[23] The heroic marks such a satire as *Mac Flecknoe*, such a biblical parallel as *Absalom and Achitophel*, numerous plays, and lyrics

such as *Alexander's Feast*. But where is Dryden's epic? The question implies a serious irony in Dryden's pretensions, one he shares with other English poets. For all except Milton found that a true, complete epic eluded them. Besides Dryden, there were Spenser, Pope, Wordsworth, and Joyce who were haunted by the heroic and yet could not create works that qualify as *Paradise Lost* qualifies.

If we know this, Dryden cannot have failed to know it of Spenser and himself. Yet he must also have known that Spenser had given the world a surrogate for a complete epic, and he tried several versions of heroic poetry himself. His earliest was either that "historical poem," *Annus Mirabilis* (1667), or that baroque curiosity, his double heroic play, *The Conquest of Granada* (1670, 1671). From there Dryden went on to *Absalom and Achitophel* (1681), which is some manner of heroic poem but to this day a work of disputed genre. Next he excerpted parts of Lucretius (1685) to make a unified collection of episodes such as that Epicurean poet had not intended.[24] Then came *The Hind and the Panther* (1687). The heroic idea informs these poems, enduring all the while an extraordinary series of transformations. It is as if Odysseus were playing Proteus. Dryden first appeared in unmistakable epic guise in his *Virgil* (1697), yet in this more than the other works just named he was mastered by the classical author. Meanwhile, a series of thinly veiled requests for support to write his own epic met with plain silence. Was there no way to create, somehow, an epic as radical as *Paradise Lost* from the materials afforded by straitened circumstances?

We know well enough what Dryden wanted to do. In his "Discourse" on satire, he speaks in more detail than formerly of his plans for an epic on one of two topics: Arthur's victory over the Saxons or the Black Prince's subduing of Spain.[25] The former was subsequently translated into *King Arthur*, with Henry Purcell the composer. As Dryden might have said, the corruption of an epic was the generation of an opera. These same plans had been set forth seventeen years before the "discourse" in the epistle dedicatory to *Aureng-Zebe* (1676). Such was the continuity of Dryden's ambition that the early dedication to John Sheffield, Earl of Mulgrave, was followed by the dedication of the *Aeneis* (1697) to the same person. The definitive study of Dryden's *Virgil* remains to be written, but it seems beyond question that it is the most important translation in the language, considering both subject and rendering. For all Dryden's alterations and adaptations, however, the design remains Virgil's. Another achievement was required

simply to enter a claim of originality sufficient for Dryden to pretend to something like *Paradise Lost*.

In that "Discourse," he makes two or three points as to his distinctive epic. The work on the Black Prince would use characters, "wherein, after Virgil and Spenser, I would have taken occasion to represent my living friends and patrons of the noblest families, and also shadowed the events of future ages, in the succession of our imperial line."[26] Dryden overrepresents the historical element in Virgil and Spenser's characters. It is as if he had planned to rewrite the *Aeneid* on the model of *Absalom and Achitophel*. Certainly it would have differed from Milton's epics. Dryden also found, like Milton, a solution to the vexed problem of "machines," those supernatural characters whom the Renaissance thought essential to epic. Out of a passage in Daniel (x, 10–21) and "the principles of Platonic philosophy as it is now Christianised," he envisioned "guardian angels." As he put it, "St Michael is mentioned by his name [in Daniel] as the patron of the Jews, and is now taken by the Christians as the protector-general of our religion." These were "tutelar genii," who "presided over the several people and regions committed to their charge."[27] Surely there is also something here of that Platonic "middle spirit," the Attendant Spirit of *Comus*, and of the Michael of *Lycidas?* Such an epic would have been patriotic, historical, explicitly Christian, and, in some fashion, allegorical. It was not to be. Instead there came the *Virgil* and, as the Preface to *Fables* shows, there would also have been a Homer had Dryden lived long enough. Indeed, that collection included as a harbinger of the Homeric poems a translation of the first book of the *Iliad*. Dryden went to his grave, and Homer was left to Pope's good offices—and very good fortune. Yet I do think that in *Fables* Dryden managed almost by accident what he had been seeking from the 1660s onward.

The *Fables* is *sui generis* in a strict sense, the epic as cento. Mingling poems to or on contemporaries with an ode like *Alexander's Feast* and with translations of Homer, Ovid, Chaucer, and Boccaccio, Dryden certainly put together an unusual collection. As I have had occasion to observe before, however, the collection is unified by links among the individual poems and by repeated treatment of several motifs and subjects.[28] Not surprisingly, the old poet who had formerly written heroic plays concerned himself with "Love" and "Arms."[29] But as *Alexander's Feast* shows— along with such extremes as *Baucis and Philemon, The Cock and the Fox,* and *Cymon and Iphigenia*—the range of love has immensely increased. Indeed, the range of all his subjects has increased by the spacious tales he retells and by their variety. I do not wonder that *Fables* was the work of Dryden's best loved by the Romantics, since I respond in the same way. He depicts in *Fables* our imperfect kind in search of the good life. Sometimes we succeed and often we fail. Usually success and failure are compounded, with the poet and the reader's shared understanding providing the norm of judgment. This appears clearly in the first "translation," *Palamon and Arcite,* in which he takes pains to stress beyond Chaucer's emphasis that as pagans the characters wander in a religious darkness. His own "English" poems provide counter-narrative elements that define the bases of human worth and of our judgment in Christian and largely contemporary terms by attention to a Duchess of Ormonde or to a Driden of Chesterton. Adapted beyond any ordinary conception of translation, the translated poems seem to distance the search for the good life, whereas the poems supplied by Dryden's own imagining approximate the remote. The effect is a universality that emerges from the extraordinary fluctuation of the relation of the characters and actions of the poems to Dryden and the reader. That universality also differs markedly from the planned epic of a patriotic, specifically Christian, historical, and allegorical cast. The cento epic represents an old and indeed dying man's compromise with exigency. It also discarded with finality the Miltonic model.

Milton had taught Dryden, but the lessons needed to be forgotten, to be transcended. Ironically, in this new heroic narrative on human worth and insufficiency, Dryden at last succeeded to the Miltonic throne of wit. Comparison was at least feasible because of difference. Milton had been the severest neoclassicist to succeed as a great English poet. He was as obsessed as Sidney or Rymer with ancient models and rules—as *Lycidas,* his two epics, *Samson Agonistes,* and his prose comments show. Milton compulsively and even ostentatiously honored the rules and models, so far so that they were rendered useless. After Milton, the neoclassical epic was possible only in translation of the great pagan works or in such splendid inverted models as *The Rape of the Lock, The Dunciad, Tom Jones,* and *Ulysses.* But Dryden was Milton's contemporary, and he could honor the poet he admired so much only by departing from him.

For reasons unknown to Clio, Dryden is usually termed the neoclassicist. Yet it is he who uses varieties of tragicomedy that shocked Sidney in principle and that Milton avoided as not allowable by the rules. Indeed it is Dryden who brings several new dramatic forms into life, including the cantata. He writes the first important praise of a city in *Annus Mirabilis*. He seldom follows available convention. Where is the perspective, the vision, the advice to a painter, the encounter with a bore, the Catholic bugaboo, the praise of beasts, and the other motifs that so mark satire by his contemporaries? Has any other poet given us two religious confessions, or religious poems of any kind at such extremes of nonfigurative and extreme fictive character? He is amazingly, constantly fertile, achieving distinction in all existing forms except prose fiction, which he approached in *An Essay of Dramatic Poesy*.

The differences between Milton and Dryden derive from profoundly variant outlooks. Milton accepts institutions such as monarchy, religion, pastoral, or epic only if the best models can be the basis of radical transformation. The one true king is divine, and the true religion is, in the end, the property solely of its deviser. On the other hand, Dryden is by nature deeply skeptical, disbelieving the perfectibility of any institution before Christ's return. Still, his support of institutions is as radically conservative as Milton's is revolutionary. Neither the revolutionary nor the conservative fills a person's whole soul, however. Dryden has a revolutionary hope for what individuals may work in change. His belief in the possibility of human progress endured many shocks and suffered revisions, but it contrasts markedly with Milton's steady adherence to the doctrine of historical decay. Milton remains suspicious of individuals, warning even Cromwell at his zenith against backsliding. In memorializing Edward King or Diodati, his central concern is with himself. In this sense, Milton is as conservative and distrustful of individuals as Dryden is hopeful. One might say of Dryden at his most conservative—say, in the Postscript to *The History of the League*—that one doubts his sympathy with any institutions other than his own, or even his ability to understand them. With Milton at his most conservative, one doubts his sympathy with, or understanding of, anybody but himself. Genuinely alternative figures such as L'Allegro and Il Penseroso were casualties of Milton's participation in the Puritan Revolution. Yet Milton's epics and Dryden's *Fables* possess the normative greatness that they do by virtue of their growing from suffering and from serious threats to ambition: only by merging their almost contrary and certainly deep-seated instincts of conservative and radical kinds did the two poets create their fullest, greatest works.

We lack adequate, simple terms to describe such counterparts. Dryden spoke of poetic families, lineal descents, and clans. To alter the proverb, it is a wise son who loves—and differs from—his father; and much the same may be said of fathers. Milton's own natural father was indulgent to him, as in his way he seems to have been in a real if patronizing degree to Dryden. Dryden's own sons and descendants—Oldham, Congreve, and Pope, for example—loved him, felt comfortable with his legacy. It tells us something of a contrary kind about Milton's austere genius—or inimitable blank verse style—that all but one of his poetic descendants came to bad ends to the extent that they emulated their forebear. Dryden is the sole exception, because he knew instinctively that Milton's blank verse was, in his figure for Shakespeare, a bow of Ulysses. Pope was saved from failure in using Milton by taking Milton on Dryden's terms.

To such understanding, Milton was a classic and a contemporary. Within ten years of the publication of *Paradise Lost* (for *The State of Innocence* in 1677), Dryden wrote that Milton's epic is "undoubtedly one of the greatest, most noble, and most sublime poems which either this age or nation has produced."[30] A classic should also have something other than superlative qualities. It should have the ability to speak to different needs, to mean different things to us during the course of our lives. Such comprehensiveness, such multifacetedness is what I take to be the import of a remark by Dryden late in life. Dennis reported that Dryden commented on his own remark just quoted. When he made it, according to Dennis, Dryden had not realized "half the extent of [Milton's] excellence."[31] Milton's greatness is testified to by poets closer to us in time than him and Dryden, as many other studies have shown, including those with which this appears. The Milton important to his contemporaries is not exactly the Milton important to the next three centuries. But Dryden's Milton matters to us in particular because it is a contemporary Milton, and a Milton to a contemporary. Because any virtue in Milton could be praised, Dryden praised those he saw. Because a classic could be used, Dryden used what he desired. Given a strong tradition of poetic kinds and of rhetorical adaptation—the traditional poetic lost only later—Dryden was able to use Milton with respect and comfort, freedom and ease. Greatness was adaptable, translatable.

Dryden himself was remarkably free from fear in contemplating or using Milton. It was the much later cult of originality that made Milton essential and destructive. The addition of that load to the burden of the past often meant a conviction of guilt in the self and in the past. So the Romantics projected their own problems onto past writers and thinkers. Whether Voltaire and Rousseau (Blake), Boileau (Keats), or Pope (Warton), it became necessary to find fathers who had eaten sour grapes in order to explain how one's own teeth had been set on edge. By the time of T. S. Eliot, Milton and Dryden were joined as guilty parties—but he could not leave either of them alone. By then, the problems of the Romantic poets had been bequeathed to post-Romantic critics. It is not the least tribute to Dryden that he recognized that *Paradise Lost* was of an order quite different from anything that had been written. Not being obsessed with a need to be original, Dryden spent about thirty years being original—and indebted to Milton as well as to other writers. Only after that long sonhood did he become completely his own man in the generous epic of his *Fables Ancient and Modern.* If imitation is the highest form of flattery, he certainly paid his tributes to Milton. But in the end, as Dryden proved, the exercise of genius is the highest tribute of all, since his *Fables* will always remain the *second* greatest narrative of the seventeenth century, the first of a few that genuinely recall *Paradise Lost* only to confirm its preeminence in our language.

Princeton University

NOTES

1. In addition to the studies cited in later notes, there are three pertinent books: Ann Ferry, *Milton and the Miltonic Dryden* (Cambridge, Mass., 1968); W. R. Parker, *Milton's Contemporary Reputation* (Columbus, Ohio, 1940; rpt. ed., Brooklyn, 1970); and John Shawcross, ed., *Milton, 1732–1801: The Critical Heritage* (London, 1972). Certain older studies retain some interest: George Sherburn, "The Early Popularity of Milton's Minor Poems," *Modern Philology*, XVII (1919, 1920), 259–78, 515–40; Ants Oras, *Milton's Editors and Commentators* (London, 1931); John Martin Telleen, *Milton dans la littérature française* (Paris, 1904); and H. Scherpbier, *Milton in Holland* (Amsterdam, 1933). Ferry's book alone is addressed to my topic and should be consulted. Better on Milton than on Dryden, it is useful but limited in the scope of its treatment of Dryden. Parker's study of Milton's reputation has but six references to Dryden; of them only two (on the "tagging" of *Paradise Lost*) draw a literary connection, and those to but a single work.

2. Christopher Ricks, "Allusion: Dryden and Pope," a lecture delivered at Princeton University, April 24, 1974, and shortly to be published. Ricks is very good on the allusive process itself.

3. Morris Freedman, "Milton and Dryden on Rhyme," *Huntington Library Quarterly*, XXIV (1961), 337. See also n. 8 below.

4. See ibid., pp. 338–39 and notes, for a detailed account.

5. Ibid., p. 343.

6. See lines 5–18. Dryden says he is shamed by Shakespeare's "godlike Romans" but says nothing about Milton.

7. *Aubrey's Brief Lives*, ed. Oliver Lawson Dick (Harmondsworth, Eng., 1962), pp. 273–74.

8. W. R. Parker, *Milton*, 2 vols. (Oxford, 1968), I, 603–04; II, 1115. See also Morris Freedman, "Dryden's Reputed Reaction to *Paradise Lost*," *N&Q*, n.s., V (1958), 14–16; and "Dryden's 'Memorable Visit' to Milton," *Huntington Library Quarterly*, XVIII (1955), 99–108. In the latter, Freedman anticipates me in stating that Milton and Dryden got on well. See also his "Milton and Dryden on Rhyme," p. 342.

9. *Brief Lives*, p. 274. It is not clear that the concatenation of paragraphs implies that Dryden frequently visited Milton.

10. See the dedicatory epistle in Dryden, *Of Dramatic Poesy and Other Critical Essays*, ed. George Watson, 2 vols. (London, 1962), I, 195, hereafter cited as Watson; and Hugh Macdonald, *John Dryden: A Bibliography* (Oxford, 1939), p. 115.

11. *The Works of John Dryden*, ed. Walter Scott, 18 vols. (London, 1808), V, 104.

12. Pierre Legouis, "Dryden plus miltonien que Milton?" reprinted in *Aspects du XVIIᵉ siècle* (Paris, 1973), pp. 159–67.

13. *Milton's Brief Epic* (Providence, R.I., 1966), chaps. 8–12.

14. *PL* VI, 746–892. My note in *The Works of John Dryden*, ed. H. T. Swedenberg, Jr., et al. (Berkeley and Los Angeles, 1969), III, 400, is in error; Dryden does not refer to Book V here. Hereafter the California edition is referred to as *Works*, and all quotations from Dryden's poetry are taken from it. Quotations from Milton's poems follow the Columbia edition, ed. Frank Allen Patterson et al. (New York, 1931).

15. *The Poetry of Meditation* (New Haven, 1954), chap. 6. For detailed discussion of the echoing, see my *Dryden's Poetry* (Bloomington, 1967), chap. 6; or my commentary on *Eleonora* in *Works*, III.

16. For one of several depictions of the scale of music, see *Dryden's Poetry*, p. 254.

17. Watson, I, 199.

18. Ibid., 207.

19. Ibid., II, 84.

20. Ibid., 150.

21. Ibid., 270–71.

22. As I have tried to emphasize in "Renaissance Contexts of Dryden's Criticism," *Michigan Quarterly Review*, XII (1973), 97–115, and in other terms in *The Restoration Mode from Milton to Dryden* (Princeton, 1974), pp. 290, 299–300.

23. See H. T. Swedenberg, Jr., "Dryden's Obsessive Concern with the Heroic," *SP*, extra no. 4 (1967), 12–26: "The evidence from the beginning to the end is everywhere" (p. 26).

24. *Works*, III, 44–66; for comment, see pp. 276–81.

25. Watson, II, 91–92.

26. Ibid., 92. Lee's poem quoted above suggests that he knew something of Dryden's epic plans long before.

27. Ibid., 88–89.

28. *Dryden's Poetry*, chap. 8. Also *The Restoration Mode*, pp. 541–56; see p. 555 for a brief comparison of Dryden's situation with that of Milton after the Restoration.

29. *To the Dutchess of Ormond*, line 6.

30. Watson, I, 196.

31. See Parker, *Milton*, I, 662. He cites John Dennis, *Original Letters* (1721), I, 75.

ON LOOKING INTO POPE'S MILTON

Barbara K. Lewalski

M Y VARIATION of Keats's title intends to recognize that I can hardly claim this essay to be a "first" look at the impact of Milton's poetry upon Pope: Raymond D. Havens and the Twickenham editors have identified and categorized large numbers of Pope's specific allusions to and echoes of Milton's poems.[1] Reuben Brower has considered how such Miltonic references intertwine with more pervasive imitations (in regard to genre, tone, metrics) of Virgil, Homer, Horace, and Dryden. And several recent critics—Douglas Knight, Aubrey Williams, Earl Wasserman, and Maynard Mack, among others—have examined the function of Miltonic allusion in individual poems.[2] My purpose here is to attempt an overall perspective on the relation of these two poets: to see what Pope thought of Milton as a poet, and in what ways— stylistic, thematic, mythopoeic—he drew upon Milton as a poetic resource. The question may also be asked in reverse: whether and how Pope's particular interests and emphases may illuminate Milton. The tentativeness of my title reflects the tentativeness of the conclusions advanced in regard to such complex issues.

Pope yields to no one in his age in the extent and soundness of his knowledge of Milton,[3] displaying throughout his lifetime an intelligent but never idolatrous admiration for many facets of Milton's genius and works. He undertook to imitate Milton's style, along with other models, in an epic project begun a little after the age of twelve; he kept Milton's picture (and later bust) in his chambers along with those of Dryden and Shakespeare; he loaned copies of Milton's poetry to friends and conversed with them about it; and he often quoted Milton in his familiar letters.[4] Havens's tables indicate over one hundred and ninety specific borrowings from Milton in at least twenty-five poems, drawn from the entire range of Milton's verse (not simply from *Paradise Lost,* as was more usual with Pope's contemporaries)—and the count has been much extended by recent editors and critics.[5]

Pope also commented upon Milton's poetic practice—especially in the epic.[6] In regard to what he considered the primary characteristic of the genius and the poet, invention, he claimed for Milton a status little inferior to that of the supreme Homer; in Milton the fire of invention "glows like a Furnace kept up to an uncommon ardor by the Force of Art."[7] In his translations of the *Iliad* and the *Odyssey* Pope annotated a number of Miltonic borrowings from Homer as well as larger stylistic debts, such as the identification of evil characters by an evaluative epithet; the characters' use of appellations of praise and honor in saluting each other; the piling of simile upon simile and the use of digressive similes to heighten an image—"a daring manner peculiar to Homer above all the ancients and Milton above all the Moderns."[8] Evaluating comparable passages, Pope sometimes awarded the laurels for poetic superiority to Homer, sometimes to Milton. Milton's catalogue of the fallen angels he commends as an imitation of Homer's catalogue of ships, but "it must be allow'd inferior."[9] On the other hand, Milton improved Homer's image of Jove's scales in the heavens weighing the fates of the Greeks and the Trojans, through his "beautiful Allusion to the Sign of *Libra* in the Heavens, and that noble Imagination of the Maker's weighing the whole World at the Creation, and all the Events of it since; so correspondent at once to Philosophy, and to the Style of the Scriptures."[10] In general, Milton's descriptions of the underworld are accorded higher praise, "as the Ideas are more noble and suitable to the characters he describes,"[11] but he disapproved equally of the raillery of Penelope's suitors and the puns of the fallen angels.[12] Pope also shows a fine awareness of Milton's imaginative adaptation of Homeric materials to his own purposes—as in the use of various parts of the Jupiter-Juno love passage from *Iliad* XIV "upon different Occasions as the Subjects of his Poem would admit": twice to express nature's joy at the congress of Adam and Eve, elsewhere to display the "lascivious Rage" of their passions after the Fall.[13]

On certain topics Pope's judgments are somewhat clouded by contemporary opinion: the narrow neoclassical principles governing his essay on pastoral poetry prevent his including *Lycidas* among the great exemplars in that kind; and he once referred to *Paradise Regained* as Milton's worst poem.[14] Somewhat more complex is his attitude toward Milton's blank verse: on various occasions he observed that, without rhyme, an uninflected language like English can be made poetic only by being "stiffened with . . . strange words" and with numerous word-order transpositions, producing a style appropriate only to a special elevated subject such as Milton's. His point seems to be that Milton does

succeed with his elevated blank-verse style, but that the achievement is well-nigh inimitable—a point he made directly to Joseph
Spence in observing that the "exotic style" of the higher parts of
Milton's poem "does very ill for others who write on natural and
pastoral subjects."[15] In sum, Pope's characteristic stance toward
Milton is one of judicious admiration and evaluation, as a passage
from his imitation of Horace's *Epistle to Augustus* indicates:

> Milton's strong pinion now not Heav'n can bound,
> Now serpent-like, in prose he sweeps the ground,
> In Quibbles, Angel and Archangel join,
> And God the Father turns a School-Divine.
> Not that I'd lop the Beauties from his book,
> Like slashing Bentley with his desp'rate Hook.[16]

The reference to "slashing Bentley" opens the issue of how
the contemporary scholar or poet ought—and ought not—to edit,
criticize, imitate, or borrow from Milton. The pedantic Richard
Bentley, who undertook to correct so-called scribal errors and ir-
regularities of diction or metrics which the blind Milton was supposedly unable to prevent or blot in his own text, is continually
scored by Pope as a horrible example of what the scholar-editor
should not do: he is "A weak officious Friend [who] becomes a
Foe"; he is "below all criticisme" as Milton is above it; he is a
"mighty Scholiast, whose unweary'd pains / Made Horace dull,
and humbled Milton's strains."[17] Pope himself had the good sense
to ignore completely the project his friend Bishop Atterbury
pressed upon him—to revise and "polish" *Samson Agonistes*—but
he did perpetrate a clever hoax upon his scholar-friend Jonathan
Richardson and the Milton editor Thomas Birch, sending them a
"Milton" sonnet of his own composition, supposedly newly discovered at Chalfont.[18]

He has nothing but scorn for the poet-imitators of Milton
who mindlessly introduce a few tags of Miltonic diction in their
poems: "with the utmost exactness and not so much as one exception, *nevertheless* was constantly *nathless; embroidered* was
broidered; hermits were *eremites; ... shady, umbrageous; ...*
nay *her* was *hir*, and *their* was *thir* through the whole poem."[19]
And in his "Postscript" to the *Odyssey* he displays a fine critical
awareness of the variety in Milton's style, wholly ignored by
such witless imitators:

The imitators of *Milton*, like most other imitators, are not *Copies* but
Caricatura's of their original; they are a hundred times more obsolete and

cramp than he, and equally so in all places: . . . *Milton* . . . is not lavish of his exotick words and phrases everywhere alike, but employs them much more where the subject is marvellous vast and strange, as in the scenes of Heaven, Hell, Chaos, etc. than where it is turn'd to the natural and agreeable, as in the pictures of Paradise, the loves of our first parents, the entertainments of Angels, and the like. . . . *Milton* has several of the latter, where we find not an antiquated affected or uncouth word, for some hundred lines together.[20]

For his own translations of Homer he justifies the use of "old Words after the manner of *Milton*" to give the *Iliad* "a venerable *Antique* Cast" and to ornament the plainer parts of the *Odyssey*.[21] Nevertheless, the criterion of contemporary standards is to be observed: the admixture of old words is not to render the language "too unfamiliar, or remote from the present purity of writing, or from that ease and smoothness which ought always to accompany Narration or Dialogue." And Milton "certainly . . . ought to be no example" when he departs from the Homeric precedent of directness and perspicuity in the dramatic speeches.[22] Pope obviously understood as well as Wordsworth or Eliot that straightforward imitation of the Miltonic style was likely to be disastrous, and he himself wisely embedded his manifold allusions and echoes and borrowings in a very different stylistic matrix.

For all that, one important use Pope made of his Miltonic borrowings (words, phrases, sentences, and longer passages) was stylistic—to supply appropriate diction, images, or tone; and at times by allusion to evoke specific Miltonic contexts for comparison and contrast. In the early poems these essentially stylistic uses predominate. Pope's *Pastorals* (1709) are replete with Miltonic words and phrases, contributing to the idealized pastoral diction and atmosphere: "bloomy Spray," "breathing Roses," "fleecy Clouds," "Amaranthine Bow'rs"—and the near-quote from *Il Penseroso* in "ev'ry Plant that drinks the Morning Dew."[23] Most striking perhaps is the echo of the familiar lines from *Lycidas*— "Rough *Satyrs* danc'd, and *Fauns* with clov'n heel / From the glad sound would not be absent long, / And old *Damaetas* lov'd to hear our song" (34–36)—in Pope's couplet, "And yet my Numbers please the rural Throng, / Rough *Satyrs* dance, and *Pan* applauds the Song" (*Summer*, 49–50). This echo, perhaps unintentionally and somewhat unfortunately, functions as an allusion evoking its context, and thereby reminds the reader of the poetic density and significance once possible to pastoral and nowhere apparent in these pretty trifles.

Pope's exercise in the genre of the Ovidian heroic epistle, *Eloisa to Abelard* (1717), draws upon Miltonic language chiefly for the creation of atmosphere—though there may be something of Webster in the mix as well, as G. Wilson Knight observed.[24] A single line, "Ye grots and caverns shagg'd with horrid thorn!" is lifted almost unaltered from *Comus*,[25] but the chief resource is *Il Penseroso* and the first ten lines of *L'Allegro*, which provide such Miltonic epithets as "uncouth cell," "brooding darkness," "low-brow'd Rocks," "twilight groves," "shadows brown," and also the description of Melancholy as a "pensive nun" with visage "O'er-laid with black," walking "with musing gait," accompanied by Contemplation and "mute Silence."[26] These echo in Pope's lines in new combinations:

> In these deep solitudes and awful cells,
> Where heav'nly-pensive, contemplation dwells,
> And ever-musing melancholy reigns;
>
> . . . .
>
> But o'er the twilight groves, and dusky caves,
> Long-sounding isles, and intermingled graves,
> Black Melancholy sits, and round her throws
> A death-like silence, and a dread repose:
>
> . . . .
>
> And low-brow'd rocks hang nodding o'er the deeps.
>
> (1–3, 163–66, 244)

In terms of style, Pope's most extensive and significant debt to Milton was contracted in the forging of an English heroic style for his translations of the *Iliad* and the *Odyssey* (1715–1726). Though these poems display many other stylistic influences—Homer himself, Virgil, Dryden's translation of the *Aeneid*, Chapman's and Madame Dacier's *Homer*[27]—and though the colloquial tone, speed, balance, and ordered expression characteristic of Pope's heroic couplets are distinctly non-Miltonic, the Milton borrowings are both very numerous and profoundly important. They add weight and dignity to the style, give flexibility to the couplet form, and provide contemporary analogues for the Homeric epithets and formulas from an already developed and still viable "English" epic language.

At the level of diction Pope makes extensive use of Milton's latinisms—words like "etherial," "involv'd," "superior," "retorted," "enormous," "incumbent"—to obtain (as Milton does) a density and layering of significance, and to give a special charge to certain common and repeated words. He also imports dozens of

Miltonic phrases and epithets unaltered or virtually so, as a kind of epic formula—"stern bespoke," "Hurl'd headlong downward," "laborious Days," "Gloomy as Night," "Earth trembled as he trod," "goary Visage," "Thick as Autumnal Leaves," "Bristled with upright Spears," "adamantine Chain," "instinct with Spirit," "Frequent and full," "various sylvan scene," "pleaded reason," "tufted trees," "cool translucent springs," "pensive steps and slow," "Painful vicissitude," "nor skill'd nor studious," "Bitter constraint," "to death devote."[28] Entire lines and longer passages from Milton also serve as epic formulas. Milton's epic question to the Heavenly Muse and the Spirit, "Say first, for Heav'n hides nothing from thy view / Nor the deep Tract of Hell," is recapitulated in Pope's rendering of the address to the Muses just before the Catalogue of Ships: "Since Earth's wide Regions, Heav'ns unmeasur'd Height, / And Hell's Abyss hide nothing from your sight." Satan "Darts his experienc't eye" through his assembled troops in Hell, and Minerva "darts her ardent Eyes" among the Grecian troops. Jove "smil'd superior" or "with superior Love" on his daughter Minerva and on Juno, even as Milton's Adam "smil'd with superior Love" on Eve. Eve is found by Satan "Veil'd in a Cloud of Fragrance" even as Jove is found by Iris and Apollo "Veil'd in a Mist of Fragrance." Satan arousing his troops from the lake of fire cries out, "Awake, arise, or be for ever fall'n," and the father of Antinous seeks to arouse Ithaca against Ulysses with much the same phrase: "Arise (or ye for ever fall) Arise!" And perhaps most amazing of all, the Miltonic formula describing unfallen Eve's response to Adam's love is employed unchanged (twice) to explain how the nymph Calypso constrained Ulysses on her island—"With sweet, reluctant, amorous delay."[29]

    The role of Milton's syntax in the formation of Pope's heroic style is less obvious but not less important. Pope's usual heroic couplet, with its end-stopped lines, its two verses or their half-lines set off in neat balance or antithesis, its caesuras marking regular pauses, its chiming end-rhymes, could easily enough prove wearying in a long poem, besides conveying a sense of patness and orderliness quite at odds with the wonder, vastness, and heroic vigor supposedly proper to epic. A couplet such as this, near the beginning of the *Iliad*, indicates where the danger might lie:

> The *Greeks* in Shouts their joint Assent declare
> The Priest to rev'rence, and release the Fair.   (I, 31–32)

The syntactical patterns borrowed from Milton provide welcome variety, dynamic movement, and some suspension of the sense of completion. One is the very common Miltonic practice of beginning a line with a verb or participial phrase, such as, in Milton, "Vaunting aloud, but rack't with deep despair"; "Wing'd with red Lightning and impetuous rage"; "Advanc't in view they stand, a horrid Front"; "Flutt'ring his pennons vain plumb down he drops" (*PL* I, 126, 175, 563; II, 933). Among Pope's imitations in this kind are: "Involv'd in Darkness lies the great Decree"; "Unstain'd with Blood his cover'd Chariots stand"; "Trembling afar th'offending pow'rs appear'd"; "Struck with amaze, yet still to doubt inclin'd" (*Iliad* I, 706; II, 942; VIII, 554; *Odyssey* V, 450). The other pattern consists of a poetic line comprising a series of polysyllabic adjectives or verbs: in Milton—"Immutable, Immortal, Infinite"; "Abortive, monstrous, or unkindly mixt"; "Unshak'n, unseduc't, unterrifi'd"; "Unpractic'd, unprepar'd, and still to seek" (*PL* III, 373, 456; V, 899; VIII, 197); and from Pope—"Confus'd, unactive, or surpriz'd with Fear"; "Pernicious, wild, regardless of the Right"; "Disgrac'd, dishonour'd, like the vilest Slave"; "But uninhabited, untill'd, unsown" (*Iliad* IV, 257; V, 1075; IX, 762; *Odyssey* IX, 143). The Miltonic effect Pope often achieves in individual lines through such syntactical techniques is quite remarkable, though of course that effect is modified with the completion of the couplet.

Yet another primarily stylistic use of Milton occurs in Pope's *Moral Essays* and *Imitations of Horace* (1731–1738), where specific echoes function as allusions, evoking Miltonic contexts for brilliant ironic or satiric effect. In his *Imitation of Horace's Second Epistle of the Second Book,* Pope's line, "The subtle Thief of Life, this paltry Time" (II, ii, 76) echoes the opening of Milton's *Sonnet VII,* "How soon hath Time, the subtle thief of youth," pointing up ironically the distance between Milton's earnest, youthful, religious anxieties about unfulfilled God-given talents and responsibilities, and the mature, urbane Pope's insistence that he has a right if he chooses to enjoy life without rhyming all the time and in unfavorable circumstances. Also invoking a Miltonic context for witty self-irony, Pope's *Imitation of Horace's Second Satire of the First Book* borrows the very line in which Adam declares ecstatically the power and uniqueness of his love for Eve— "Transported I behold, / Transported touch" (VIII, 529–30)—to express the disenchanted, worldly-wise speaker's willingness to settle for any "willing Nymph" who is clean and tolerably fair (*Serm.* I, ii, 165). We find a satiric use of Miltonic allusion in the

Epistle to Bathurst, as Satan's first words to Beelzebub in Hell echo in the description of Buckingham on his sordid deathbed— "Great Villiers lies—alas! how chang'd from him"—and thereby relate Buckingham to his demonic original.[30] The same point is insinuated more wittily in the line from the *Epistle to Dr. Arbuthnot*—"Or at the Ear of Eve, familiar Toad" (319)—relating the flattering toady, Lord Hervey (Sporus in the poem) to Milton's unforgettable image of Satan, "Squat like a Toad, close at the ear of Eve" (IV, 800). On other occasions the Miltonic allusions work as parody, pointing the satire by the discrepancy between the Miltonic context and Pope's application. In the "Timon's Villa" section of the *Epistle to Burlington,* the line from *Il Penseroso* describing the religious ecstasies afforded to the contemplative recluse, "And bring all Heav'n before mine eyes" (166) is twice parodied: Timon's tastelessly grandiose estate "brings all Brobdignag before your thought" (104), and the garishly painted ceiling in his chapel, with its sprawling saints on gilded clouds, will "bring all Paradise before your eye" (148) in a synthetic baroque substitute for mystical vision. Or again, in the *Epilogue to the Satires, Dialogue I,* Pope's line, "All Tears are wip'd for ever from all Eyes" (102), at once describes and passes judgment upon the *"sweet Nepenthe"* of the court where successful courtiers and ministers forget all sense of human misery, as the *Lycidas* allusion recalls that poem's true transcendence won through unshrinking confrontation with human misery, pain, and mortality.[31]

    Pope's *Essay on Man* (1733–1734) is set forth explicitly as a theodicy, and the opening lines invite a direct comparison of its argument with that of *Paradise Lost.* The "scene of Man" Pope proposes to reflect upon is described as either "A Wild" or (in Miltonic terms) as a "Garden, tempting with forbidden fruit"; the analysis of the subject is introduced with a formula, "Say first, of God above or Man below," which is reminiscent of Milton's epic question. And the statement of purpose—"Laugh where we must, be candid where we can; / But vindicate the ways of God to Man"—repeats Milton's familiar statement almost verbatim.[32] At the same time the argument is transposed to a new key: Reuben Brower notes the vast discrepancy of tone between Milton's epic proposition and Pope's "chummy, clubby ... worldly invitation to 'laugh' or view with generosity," underscored by the significant shift from the Miltonic term *justify* used in a prayer— "that ... / I may assert Eternal Providence, / And [may] justify"—

to Pope's "vindicate," which evokes the atmosphere of debate and points scored.[33]

As several recent critics have observed, though some of the topics Pope addresses have contemporary analogues and perhaps sources in Bolingbroke, Shaftesbury, Archbishop William King, and others, many are central to the tradition of Renaissance Christian humanism. Pope's statement of these topics, especially in view of the Miltonic context set by the opening lines, often recalls Milton's formulation of these same commonplaces.[34] One such topic in the *Essay on Man* concerns the vital divine impulse permeating the entire creation, whose parts are precisely ordered according to "just gradation," in a vast, hierarchical Chain of Being:

> See, thro' this air, this ocean, and this earth,
> All matter quick, and bursting into birth.
> . . . .
> All are but parts of one stupendous whole,
> Whose body Nature is, and God the soul;
> . . . .
> What'er of life all-quick'ning aether keeps,
> Or breathes thro' air, or shoots beneath the deeps,
> Or pours profuse on earth; one nature feeds
> The vital flame, and swells the genial seeds.
>   (I, 233–34, 267–68; III, 115–18)

This language, and the speaker's sense of wonder and amazement, owe something to the marvelous vitality of Milton's Creation account, with its pervasive imagery of procreation, generation, the infusing of vital warmth into all things, and the springing of all beings to birth (*PL* VII, 243–534), and perhaps still more to Raphael's explanation to Adam of the nature of nature:

> O *Adam*, one Almighty is, from whom
> All things proceed, and up to him return,
> If not deprav'd from good, created all
> Such to perfection, one first matter all,
> Indu'd with various forms, various degrees
> Of substance, and in things that live, of life;
> But more refin'd, more spiritous, and pure,
> As nearer to him plac't or nearer tending
> Each in thir several active Spheres assign'd,
> Till body up to spirit work, in bounds
> Proportion'd to each kind.   (V, 469–79)

Pope's memorable formulation of the blasphemy of seeking to understand and challenge God's universal order:

> Is the great chain, that draws all to agree,
> And drawn supports, upheld by God, or thee?
> . . . .
> Snatch from his hand the balance and the rod,
> Re-judge his justice, be the GOD of GOD!
>
>   (I, 33–34, 121–22)

recalls Abdiel's challenge to Satan:

> Shalt thou give Law to God, shalt thou dispute
> With him the points of liberty, who made
> Thee what thou art, and form'd the Pow'rs of Heav'n
> Such as he pleas'd, and circumscrib'd thir being?   (V, 822–25)

Pope's central proposition is of course that the proper focus for human inquiry is human nature and the conditions of human life:

> The bliss of Man (could Pride that blessing find)
> Is not to act or think beyond mankind;
> No pow'rs of body or of soul to share,
> But what his nature and his state can bear.
> . . . .
> Know then thyself, presume not God to scan;
> The proper study of Mankind is Man.   (I, 189–92; II, 1–2)

This formulation recalls Raphael's advice to Adam during the discourse on astronomy:

> Solicit not thy thoughts with matters hid;
> Leave them to God above . . .
>   joy thou
> In what he gives to thee, this Paradise
> And thy fair *Eve:* Heav'n is for thee too high
> To know what passes there; be lowly wise;
> Think only what concerns thee and thy being.
>
>   (VIII, 167–74)

On the basis of such analogues, Maynard Mack views Pope's poem as virtually a redaction of the argument of *Paradise Lost,* transposed from narrative, myth, and allegory to abstract terms:

As every one knows, the central conflict in Milton's epic is that between the hierarchical order, coherence, law, love, harmony, unity, and happiness of a world created and sustained according to God's purposes, and the chaos, rebellion, dissension, hatred, and misery brought into it by man's and Satan's unwillingness to be contented with these purposes and their part in them. . . . Pope manages to precipitate a meaning that, like Milton's, is in one sense the story of a conflict between religious humility and irreligious pride, and in another sense, the story of universal order, the ways it can be violated, and the ways it must be restored. . . . Beginning with a reminder of a paradise man has lost, the poem ends with a paradise he can regain.[35]

To this impressive summary, however, it is necessary to enter a qualification: Pope not only responds to and abstracts, but also significantly alters, Milton's themes. The chief tenet of Pope's theodicy is, "All partial Evil, universal Good"—that is, whatever we perceive as evil from our limited perspective and in relation to some parts of the creation must be understood as working to the greatest possible good of the whole, "May, must be right, as relative to all." From that vantage point, "Whatever is, is Right."[36] The chief argument of Milton's theodicy is twofold: that evil originates in the perversion by free agents of God's good creation, and that the creative energy of God continually brings greater good out of evil. In Pope's argument evil, from the divine perspective, does not exist; in Milton's it most assuredly does: it is in constant, dynamic opposition to good throughout history, but will ultimately be overcome. Even the central terms in the two arguments carry different thematic import. Hierarchy for Pope is absolute, fixed, static, immutable: the different species are "for ever sep'rate, yet for ever near," and middle natures nearly meet "Yet never pass th'insuperable line." For Milton the hierarchical order is curiously fluid and dynamic: the various entities are "more refin'd, more spiritous, and pure, / As nearer to him [God] plac't *or nearer tending*"; among rational creatures (men and angels) the intellectual processes are different "but in degree, of kind the same"; and unfallen men are invited to contemplate progressive refinement to angelic condition.[37] Pride is the cardinal evil in both systems, but for Pope it is principally a matter of the intellect—"In Pride, in reas'ning Pride, our error lies"—whereas in Milton it arises essentially from the perverse will.[38] And reason itself plays a significantly different role in the two poems. In the *Essay on Man* it gives some check and direction to the character-determining ruling passion, but chiefly promotes submission to God's vast incomprehensible plan—"To Reason right is to submit" (I, 164, II, 53–80). In *Paradise Lost* it directs the continuous dynamics of free choice through which alone potentialities for good or for evil are actualized throughout the creation and in man—"Reason also is choice," declares Milton's God (III, 108).

Much the most interesting of Pope's uses of Milton are those in which he calls upon and reworks Milton's mythopoesis in the creation of his own myths—for public panegyric once, but most impressively and characteristically for satiric purposes. *Windsor-Forest* (1713) specifically invites comparison of its groves with "the Groves of *Eden*" and draws upon *topoi* from Milton's Eden as well as from the *Georgics,* Alcinous' garden, and the pastoral landscapes of Milton's early verse to suggest that England under the Stuarts was, so far as postlapsarian conditions permit, a new Eden, a Golden Age restored.[39] In a very different vein, in *The Rape of the Lock* (1714) Miltonic myth fuses with elements from Homer, Virgil, and Dryden's Virgil to produce a flawless mock-epic, bringing exalted epic conventions to bear upon a subject of utter though charming triviality. At the same time, however, the association of Milton's mythic universe with Pope's intimates with the utmost delicacy a level of seriousness to this frothy affair, which becomes in one dimension a comic replay of the Fall.

As Aubrey Williams, Cleanth Brooks, and several others have suggested, Belinda is in some sense an Eve-figure.[40] In her morning dream inspired by her guardian sylph, Ariel, he addresses her as "Fairest of Mortals, thou distinguish'd Care / Of thousand bright Inhabitants of Air! / . . . Thy own Importance know, / Nor bound thy narrow Views to Things below" (I, 27–28, 35–36). These lines recall Eve's dream in which Satan urged her to "Ascend to Heav'n, by merit thine" (V, 80), and play off against Raphael's advice to Adam, "Heav'n is for thee too high / To know what passes there . . . / Think only what concerns thee and thy being" (VIII, 172–74). Belinda at her dressing table bending before the "heav'nly Image in the Glass" (I, 125) recalls Eve in her narcissistic posture reaching out to her own image in the pool (IV, 460–66); Belinda's "mazy Ringlets" (II, 139) recall Eve's "wanton ringlets" (IV, 306); and Belinda also has a foe resolved (as Satan was) to win by "Fraud or Force." (*RL* II, 34; *PL* II, 41). Moreover, as Eve aspired to be a god, so Belinda assumes the role of goddess—worshiping herself on her dressing-table altar, and "creating" the world of ombre in a brilliant parody of the diving *Fiat Lux*—"*Let Spades be Trumps!* she said, and Trumps they were."[41] Further ambiguities are introduced by Miltonic allusions relating the sylphs both to the faithful and the fallen angels. Like Satan carved by Michael's sword, a sylph severed by the Baron's shears finds that his "Airy Substance soon unites again"; like the angelic protectors of Eden, the sylphs' protective power over Belinda lasts only as long as her state of innocence (that is, coquetry) is preserved; and like the angels of both sorts, they "Assume what Sexes and what Shapes they please." And amusingly enough, Ariel's address to his forces, "Ye *Sylphs* and *Sylphids,* to

your Chief give Ear, / *Fays Fairies, Genii, Elves,* and *Daemons*
hear," parodies a line found both in God's and in Satan's addresses
to their respective angelic troops: "Thrones, Dominations, Prince-
doms, Virtues, Powers."[42]

Though these allusions serve chiefly, of course, to enhance
the comedy by comparing small things with great, they also play
several not entirely frivolous variations upon Milton's myth of the
Fall. Belinda and Ariel's version of the state of innocence (perfect
coquetry) is itself a form of that false chastity denounced by Milton in his celebration of the wedded love of Adam and Eve, and
the sylphs' services to Belinda (the dream, the dressing-table rites)
are also a temptation to pride. Accordingly, what Ariel perceives
as Belinda's fall—her susceptibility to thoughts of a human lover—
we may see as an accession of virtue, or at least humanity. The
rape of the lock of hair, the external emblem of the perfect state of
coquetry, is a fall in reputation which turns Belinda into a "degraded toast" for Thalastris and others who judge honor solely by
appearances. In this situation, Clarissa's appeal to good sense,
good humor, and merit as the true basis for honor transposes to
appropriate feminine terms Sarpedon's speech in the *Iliad,* and
also Michael's advice to Adam on the achievement of true inner
virtue in the fallen state.[43] But Belinda cannot rise to this challenge and instead succumbs to spleen. This is the true "fall,"
carrying with it its own punishment—the transformation of the
charming Belinda into a scold and virago, and of the decorous
drawing-room battle of the sexes into a sexual free-for-all: "That
single Act gives half the World the Spleen" (IV, 78). Pope's cau-
tionary tale for Arabella Fermor derives much of its fun and some
of its point by playing so skillfully off Milton's central myth.

The *Dunciad* in the final, four-book version (1743) contains
Pope's most extensive, most significant, and most creative use of
Milton's myths. The earlier three-book *Dunciad* with its clear parody of the epic proposition of the *Aeneid*—"Books and the Man I
sing, the first who brings / The Smithfield Muses to the Ear of
Kings"—is essentially a mock-epic, with Theobald a duncely Aeneas transferring Dulness's kingdom from city to court.[44] Though
some residue of this material and tone remain in the revised version, Pope's new epic statement identifies the Goddess Dulness as
the principal agent—"The Mighty Mother and her Son"—and
Pope's footnote confirms a new subject: "The main action of the
Poem [is] . . . the Restoration of the Empire of Dulness."[45] The
new focus brings Miltonic materials pertaining to Chaos, Ancient

Night, God, the Son, and Satan into prominence, moving the poem to a new generic identification. The subject, defined through these materials, is nothing less than the decline and final demise of civilization and all human values, the regression, disordering, and uncreation of all things and their incorporation again into the realm of Chaos and Night. Despite the comic situations and the often bathetic style, this is no longer mock-epic: it is at least in part an anti-epic or demonic epic, a *Paradise Lost* with the dark powers wholly triumphant and—except for the manifestation the poem itself makes of the counterforce of wit—with no vision of countervailing creative power or of ultimate restoration.[46]

The basis for Pope's poem is Milton's invented myth of Satan's offer to help the Anarch Chaos regain that portion of his realm taken over by the created universe (*PL* II, 959–1010). The Anarch and his consort Ancient Night receive little development as personages in Milton's poem, but the realm of Chaos is very important—as the substratum of all things, as the condition of limitless possibility where all things are "in thir pregnant causes mixt / Confus'dly," as "The Womb of nature and perhaps her Grave" (II, 911–14). In Milton's prelapsarian universe the destructive potential of Chaos is checked and bounded by the active creative power of God (symbolized often by Light), by the orderly processes of nature, and by the governance exercised by man— imaged by the gardening activities of Adam and Eve; Satan must therefore take the initiative with the Anarch. After the Fall the ordering processes are greatly disrupted, and Pope's revision of Milton's myth develops the full implications of postlapsarian disorder. The Goddess Dulness, daughter of Chaos and Ancient Night and thereby the primary manifestation of their essential natures and qualities in the human world, is now the prime mover, sending forth her emissary to further her kingdom—and that of her parents. Darkness and disorder, sheer entropy—in the absence of the ordering and civilizing power of true art, reason, principled government, sound education, discriminating language—are about to take over and destroy the world.

Though the general association of Dulness and the Dunces with Milton's Chaos and Satan has been much discussed,[47] it is worth noting precisely how the mythic materials are adapted. Besides manifesting in human terms the disorder and darkness inherited from Chaos and Night, the Goddess Dulness also parodies the nature and actions of Milton's God and his Son: This "Mighty Mother" shines "In clouded Majesty" and "A veil of fogs dilates her awful face" (I, 45, 262) even as Milton's Almighty Father can only be seen "through a cloud" (III, 378). Also, like Milton's God she creates and pronounces her creation good—"With self-applause her wild creation views"—and she also takes delight in all who express her image, especially her son Cibber: "In each she marks her Image full exprest, / But chief in BAYS's monster-breeding breast" (I, 82, 107–08). Termed the "Antichrist of Wit," Cibber is defined through allusion both to Milton's Satan and to the Christ of *Paradise Lost* and *Paradise Regained*. His thinking processes are described in the imagery of Satan's flight through Chaos: "Sinking from thought to thought, a vast profound! / Plung'd for his sense, but found no bottom there."[48] Parodying the sacrificial role of the Son in *Paradise Lost,* Cibber's sacrifice of his own abortive works and the books from which he plundered them proves his worthiness to be King and Messiah, and Dulness so proclaims him: "My son! the promis'd land expects thy reign / . . . Lift up your gates, ye Princes, see him come" (I, 292, 301). He is crowned in the Dome of Dulness, which owes much to Milton's Paradise of Fools, and is enthroned, like Satan, "High on a gorgeous seat" to view epic games celebrating his coronation.[49] These games, degraded to comic horseplay, occasionally echo their ultimate source in Milton's Chaos.[50]

At length, sunk in oblivion on Dulness's lap, Cibber dreams an encounter with his poetic father Settle (parodying that of Aeneas with Anchises) and enjoys a vision of the coming glories of his reign. Again, Miltonic contexts which comment on that reign are supplied through allusions to Adam's vision of the sad future of the world occasioned by his sin, and to Christ's prospect of the Kingdoms of the World proffered in Satan's temptation.[51] These motifs culminate in Book IV, which is at once an Honors Day at court, a "Triumph" of the Goddess Dulness, a version of Milton's Council in Hell, and a parody Last Judgment as described by Michael to Adam, in which the Son will come "To judge th' unfaithful dead, but to reward / His faithful," and will produce "New Heav'ns, new Earth, Ages of endless date / Founded in righteousness and peace and love" (*PL* XII, 461–62, 549–50). The Goddess Dulness here takes on the role of the Son at the Second Coming: science, wit, logic, rhetoric, the muses, and all varieties of good knowledge are chained beneath her throne in punishment; the witless of "all the nations" come to receive commendation for their respective varieties of dullness; and the goddess prepares "Of dull and venal a new World to mold" (IV, 15, 72).

The opening lines, in which the poet presents himself as inevitably subject to the forces his poem celebrates, ring startling changes upon the great invocations of Milton's epic bard—in Book I to the Spirit who presided at the Creation, to order his Chaos and enlighten his darkness, and in Book III, to the Holy Light in thanksgiving for his escape from the "darkness visible" of Hell and the Night of Chaos, and in petition for inner illumination: "the mind through all her powers / Irradiate, there plant eyes, all mist from thence / Purge and disperse, that I may see and tell / Of things invisible to mortal sight" (III, 52–55). Pope's bard begs:

> Yet, yet a moment, one dim Ray of Light
> Indulge, great Chaos, and eternal Night!
> Of darkness visible so much be lent,
> As half to shew, half veil the deep Intent.
> Ye Pow'rs! whose Mysteries restor'd I sing,
> To whom Time bears me on his rapid wing,
> Suspend a while your Force inertly strong,
> Then take at once the Poet and the Song.   (IV, 1–8)

Before the throne come many trailing their Miltonic contexts. The schoolmaster (Busby of Westminster) claims his due reward as a Moloch: "His beaver'd brow a birchen garland wears, / Dropping with Infant's blood, and Mother's tears."[52] The university pedant and foolish critic (Bentley, who "humbled Milton's strains") assumes the grave stance of a Beelzebub: "Plow'd was his front with many a deep Remark"; his special contributions to the kingdom are the dissociation of words from things and things from their uses, together with the promulgation of "much Divinity without a *Nous*."[53] One of the "Virtuosi" (narrow experimenters who see and seek nothing outside their narrow spheres) is a butterfly collector who defines his activity by a telling echo of Eve's narcissistic pursuit of her own image: "It fled, I follow'd; now in hope, now pain; / It stopt, I stopt; it mov'd, I mov'd again."[54] A youth just returned from the Grand Tour is presented to the goddess, like the children in *Comus* to their parents, by an "Attendant Orator"—but unlike Milton's Lady, this "accomplish't Son" has "gather'd every Vice" and indulged every sensual temptation offered him on his journey (IV, 281–334). The perversion of religion is the province of the irreligious skeptic who, in imitation of Satan entering Eden, will "at one bound o'er-leaping all his laws, / Make God Man's Image, Man the final Cause."[55] At length the goddess sends forth her forces to take over all the earth, but her nod effects the cataclysm more appropriately. The final, tremendous lines gain part of their power by their explicit reversal of the vital creative force and glorious power of light, divine and human, celebrated throughout *Paradise Lost,* and also by their reversal of the final myth of the Nativity Ode, in which all the powers associated in any degree with the darkness flee before the dawning light of the Incarnate Christ:

> She comes! she comes! the sable Throne behold
> Of *Night* Primaeval, and of *Chaos* old!
> Before her, Fancy's gilded clouds decay,
> And all its varying Rain-bows die away.
> *Wit* shoots in vain its momentary fires,
> The meteor drops, and in a flash expires.
> · · · · · · · ·
> *Art* after *Art* goes out, and all is Night.
> See skulking *Truth* to her old Cavern fled,
> Mountains of Casuistry heap'd o'er her head!
> · · · · · · · ·
> *Religion* blushing veils her sacred fires,
> And unawares *Morality* expires.
> Nor *public* Flame, nor *private,* dares to shine;
> Nor *human* Spark is left, nor Glimpse *divine!*
> Lo! thy dread Empire, CHAOS! is restor'd;
> Light dies before thy uncreating word:
> Thy hand, great Anarch! lets the curtain fall;
> And universal Darkness buries All.   (IV, 629–56)

From all this it will be evident that Pope's extensive, intelligent, and creative use of Milton is a tribute of the highest order. There is no evidence here of the dark Oedipal anxieties and desperate Satanic resolutions which Harold Bloom has recently offered as a paradigm for the relations of poetic fathers and sons— a paradigm which, one suspects, pertains only to Romantic or post-Romantic poets, and only to a few of those.[56] At any rate, Pope was clearly capable of admiring, learning from, and borrowing from Milton's poetry without forcing himself into Milton's image, or Milton into his.

If we turn the perspective glass for a moment, the consideration of Milton in terms of Pope's interests and emphases may bring into focus aspects of his work somewhat scanted by our usual approaches. In the first place we will recognize that the question of Homer's large impact—conceptually and stylistically— upon Milton's tragic epic has yet to be thoroughly examined, and that Pope's own annotations and comments might serve as an appropriate starting point for that undertaking. Again, Pope's special concerns may remind us how much of moral essay and philosophical disquisition there is in *Paradise Lost*—in Raphael's discourses on the nature of being, on the cosmic system, and on the limits of human knowledge; in the Father's exposition of foreknowledge and free will; in the debate between Abdiel and Satan on the sources of political rule and the nature of tyranny—as well as throughout *Paradise Regained* in the exchanges between Christ and Satan on true and false kingship, glory, and wisdom. Milton has provided an important model for the poetry of ideas and argument, as this retrospective glance shows.

In addition, this exercise may extend our awareness of the large component of satire in Milton's epics—a feature Pope himself identified in his observation that alone among the moderns Milton followed Homer in including "ludicrous descriptions" in epic.[57] The varieties of Miltonic satire include the "ludicrous descriptions" of the Paradise of Fools and of Satan's victory rally in Hell transformed to a chorus of hissing snakes; the mock-epic features (bathos, ludicrous situations, parody, outrageous puns) of the War in Heaven and the encounter between Sin, Death, and Satan at Hell's Gate; the invective of Adam's denunciation of Eve after the Fall, and of Christ's denunciation of would-be world conquerors in *Paradise Regained;* the imitative irony of the bumbling speech of the Anarch Chaos; the "derisive" irony of the Father's comments upon the approaching Satanic armies; the dramatic irony of Adam's constant misapprehension of what he sees during Michael's presentation of future history to him; and especially the satiric mimesis of the misuse of language, the debasement of rhetoric, the perversion of reason by illogic and delusion in the political oratory of Hell and in the speech of postlapsarian human beings. Pope may well remind us how impressive a model Milton provided for serious poetic satire.

Moreover, we may appreciate how much of Pope's anti-epic of dullness, darkness, and disorder is implicit in Milton's portrayal of Chaos and Ancient Night: in the first vision of the tiny created universe hanging by a slender chain in the midst of the swirling abyss of Chaos; in the fearful encroachments of Chaos upon the universe and man after the Fall; in the altogether surprising insistence upon the necessity of Adam and Eve's gardening activities to control unruly growth even in the prelapsarian Eden. Pope's question is already implicit in Milton: What if the creative, ordering forces of God and man ceased to operate or to be effective? Recognition of that dimension may enhance our sense of the complexity of Milton's vision and of his myth making.

The double perspective also reveals—and underscores the

value of—the Milton Pope does not and cannot use. After reading through forty-eight books of epic heroic couplets, we may applaud more vigorously than ever the cogency of Milton's argument for blank verse over rhyme in epic, and the skill with which he solved the problems (so clearly recognized by Pope) which that choice posed for the poet writing in an uninflected language. At another level, we cannot but be impressed by the greater inclusiveness of Milton's vision: his unflinching recognition of evil as evil; his presentation of Chaos not only as the power of disintegration and disorder but also as the source and substratum of all creation, emanating originally from God; his conception of hierarchy as fluid and dynamic rather than fixed and static. Moreover, this exercise highlights the central importance for Milton of man's responsibility to order himself and his world. Displaying, as Pope does, the fragility and the limitations of human faculties, and emphasizing much more vigorously than Pope the power and subtlety of evil, Milton yet demands that human beings see themselves as sufficient to stand, able to choose, and responsible for the consequences of their choices. Finally, recognizing Pope's large capacity to assimilate (even as Milton did before him) the classical, European, and English cultural traditions in the creation of his poetry yet to find his own perspective upon it and his own poetic voice, we must see that Milton's poetic undertaking was bolder still: not only to assimilate, use, and rework but also in his great epic to surpass the highest poetic achievements of that tradition. In sum, looking back at Milton through a lens revealing Pope's pervasive sense of human weakness, folly, vice, irrationality, philistinism, and affinity for the powers of darkness and disorder, we might again be struck with amazement (like stout Cortez upon that peak) at the daring and splendor of Milton's vision of the boundless creativity and dynamic ordering power of God, man, and poetry.

Brown University

NOTES

1. All quotations from Pope's poetry are from the Twickenham edition, *The Poems of Alexander Pope*, ed. John Butt, 10 vols. (London, 1950–67). All quotations from Milton's poetry are from *John Milton: Complete Poems and Major Prose*, ed. Merritt Y. Hughes (New York, 1957). Havens, *The Influence of Milton on English Poetry* (Cambridge, Mass., 1922), pp. 113–118, 573–83.

2. Brower, *Alexander Pope: The Poetry of Allusion* (Oxford, 1968); Knight, *Pope and the Heroic Tradition* (New Haven, 1951); Williams, "The 'Fall' of China and *The Rape of the Lock*," *PQ*, XLI (1962), 412–25; Williams, *Pope's* Dunciad: *A Study of Its Meaning* (London, 1955); Wasserman, "The Limits of Allusion in *The Rape of the Lock*," *JEGP*, LXV (1966), 425–44; and Mack, "Introduction," *An Essay on Man*, Twickenham, III, pt. 1, xlvii–lxxx.

3. For a broad sample of contemporary opinion of Milton, see John Shawcross, ed., *Milton: The Critical Heritage* (London, 1970); and idem, *Milton, 1732–1801: The Critical Heritage* (London, 1972).

4. See *The Correspondence of Alexander Pope*, ed. George Sherburn, 5 vols. (Oxford, 1956), esp. the following letters: Sir William Trumbull to Pope, October 19, 1705 (I, 10); Pope to Caryll, June 25, 1711 (I, 120); Pope to Caryll, December 21, 1712 (I, 166–68); Pope to Tonson, Sr., June 7, 1732 (III, 291); and Pope to Edward Blount, October 21, 1721 (II, 88–89). See also Joseph Spence, *Observations, Anecdotes, and Characters of Books and Men Collected from Conversation*, ed. James M. Osborn, 2 vols. (Oxford, 1966), items 40, 57 (I, 18, 25).

5. Havens, *Influence of Milton*, p. 114.

6. Some of these points have been noted in Austin Warren's fine book, *Pope as Critic* (Princeton, 1929).

7. "Preface" to the *Iliad*, ed. Maynard Mack (Twickenham, VII, 5).

8. Notes to *Iliad* I, 33, 97; II, 950; XIII, 384 (Twickenham, VII, 87, 91, 168–69; VIII, 123–25). My examples are drawn chiefly from the *Iliad;* I have largely avoided in subsequent documentation those books of the *Odyssey* for which Pope delegated responsibility to Broome and Fenton, though of course he did oversee the whole and so bears final responsibility for the entire text and apparatus.

9. *Observations on the Catalogue* (Twickenham, VII, 176); cf. *Iliad* II, 586 ff., *PL* I, 392 ff.

10. Note to *Iliad* VIII, 88 (Twickenham, VII, 399–401); cf. *PL* IV, 996–1004.

11. Note to *Iliad* II, 939; *Odyssey* XI, 701 (Twickenham, VII, 168; IX, 419–20); cf. *PL* II, 528–55.

12. Notes to *Iliad* XVI, 904; *Odyssey* XVIII, 470 (Twickenham, VII, 278–79; X, 191).

13. Note to *Iliad* XIV, 395 (Twickenham, VII, 181–82). Pope compares *Iliad* XIV, 395–404 to *PL* VIII, 510–17, and *PL* IV, 698–702; also *Iliad* XIV, 355–406, to *PL* IX, 1029–45. He notes also the transformation of Homer's Sleep in the likeness of a Bird on the Fir-Tree of Mount Ida (XIV, 327–28) to Satan in the likeness of a Cormorant on the Tree of Life (*PL* IV, 194–96).

14. *A Discourse on Pastoral Poetry* (Twickenham, I, 23–33). By Pope's standards, several of Virgil's and Spenser's eclogues are also excluded. The comment on *Paradise Regained* is in a letter to Atterbury, March 19, 1721/22, in *Correspondence*, II, 110.

15. See Pope's observations in the preface to Parnell's version of *Homer's "Battle of the Frogs and Mice"* (London, 1717), cited in Knight, *Heroic Tradition*, pp. 62–63; Spence, *Observations*, items 395, 459 (I, 173, 197).

16. *Epis.* II, i, 99–104 (Twickenham, IV, 203).

17. "Occasion'd by seeing some Sheets of Dr. B--TL-Y's Edition of Milton's *Paradise Lost*," line 4, in *Epigrams from The Grub-Street Journal*, VIII (Twickenham, VI, 328); letter to Tonson, Sr., June 7, 1732, in *Correspondence*, III, 291; *Dunciad* IV, 211–12 (Twickenham, V, 363).

18. Atterbury to Pope, June 15, 1722, in *Correspondence*, II, 124–25; Pope to

Jonathan Richardson, July 18, 1737, ibid., IV, 80–81. Explanation of the hoax occurs in a letter from George Vertue to the Earl of Oxford, February 27, 1737/38, cited in Sherburn's note to Pope's letter of July 18, 1737.

19. *Peri Bathous: Of the Art of Sinking in Poetry* (1728), in *Literary Criticism of Alexander Pope*, ed. Bertrand A. Goldgar (Lincoln, Nebr., 1965), p. 62.

20. Twickenham, X, 390–91.

21. "Preface" to the *Iliad* (Twickenham, VII, 19); "Postscript" to the *Odyssey* (Twickenham, X, 390).

22. "Postscript" to the *Odyssey* (ibid., 390–91).

23. *Spring*, 23, and Milton, *Sonnet I*, 1; *Spring*, 32, and Milton, *Arcades*, 32; *Autumn*, 14, and *Il Penseroso*, 72; *Winter*, 73, and *PL* XI, 77–78; *Summer*, 32, and *Il Penseroso*, 172, "And every Herb that sips the dew."

24. G. Wilson Knight, *The Burning Oracle* (Oxford, 1939), pp. 148–55.

25. Line 20; cf. *Comus*, 429, "By grots and caverns shagg'd with horrid shades."

26. *L'Allegro*, 5, 6, 8; *Il Penseroso*, 133, 134, 16, 31–55.

27. For a discussion of these various influences, see Brower, *Poetry of Allusion*, pp. 85–141; Maynard Mack's "Introduction" to the Homer translations (Twickenham, VII, xlix–ccxlix); and Knight, *Heroic Tradition*, pp. 34–81.

28. *Iliad* V, 1093, and *Lycidas*, 112; *Iliad* I, 761, and *PL* I, 45; *Iliad* IX, 431, and *Lycidas*, 72; *Iliad* XII, 554, and *PL* VI, 832; *Iliad* XIII, 30, and *PL* II, 676; *Iliad* XIII, 272, and *Lycidas*, 62; *Iliad* II, 970, and *PL* I, 302; *Iliad* XIII, 431, and *PL* VI, 82; *Iliad* XIII, 452, and *PL* I, 48; *Iliad* XVIII, 442, and *PL* VI, 752; *Iliad* XIX, 48, XXIII, 38, and *PL* I, 797; *Odyssey* V, 80, and *PL* IV, 140; *Odyssey* V, 455, VII, 308, and *PL* VIII, 510; *Odyssey* V, 513, X, 176, and *L'Allegro*, 78; *Odyssey* VII, 231, X, 434, and *Comus*, 86; *Odyssey* X, 286, XIII, 235, and *PL* XII, 648, IV, 173; *Odyssey* I, 152, and *PL* VI, 8; *Odyssey* I, 261, and *PL* IX, 42; *Odyssey* I, 300, and *Lycidas*, 6; *Odyssey* XX, 423, and *PL* IX, 901.

29. *PL* I, 27–28, and *Iliad* II, 574–75; *PL* I, 568, and *Iliad* II, 525; *Iliad* VIII, 48, XIV, 387, and *PL* IV, 499; *PL* IX, 425, and *Iliad* XV, 174; *PL* I, 330, and *Odyssey* XXIV, 497; *Odyssey* I, 22, IX, 32, and *PL* IV, 311.

30. *PL* I, 84–85; *Moral Essays* III, 305.

31. *Lycidas*, 181, "And wipe the tears for ever from his eyes."

32. *Essay on Man* I, 1–16; *PL* I, 1–27. For some discussion of the *Essay* as a response to Milton, see David P. French, "Pope, Milton, and the *Essay on Man*," *Bucknell Review*, XVI (1968), 103–11.

33. Brower, *Poetry of Allusion*, pp. 207–08.

34. For a careful analysis of the claims—and qualifications upon the claims—made for these various influences, see Maynard Mack's "Introduction" to Twickenham, III, pt. 1, xxvi–lxiii.

35. Ibid., pp. liii–lxiii.

36. *Essay on Man*, I, 52, 292–94. For a fine discussion of the differing implications of this argument from the divine and the human perspectives, see Isabel Rivers, *The Poetry of Conservatism, 1600–1745* (Cambridge, 1973), pp. 182–86.

37. *Essay on Man* I, 224, 228; *PL* V, 476 (emphasis added); *PL* V, 490, 496–501.

38. *Essay on Man* I, 123; cf. *PL* V, 809–12.

39. *Windsor-Forest*, 7–10; see also 30, 38, 118; and *PL* IV, 248, 149; VII, 434. Other Miltonic echoes include "checquer'd Scene" (*WF*, 17) and "Checquer'd shade" (*L'Allegro*, 96); "tufted Trees" (*WF*, 27) and *L'Allegro*, 78. "The gulphy *Lee* his sedgy Tresses rears" (*WF*, 346) and "gulphie Dun," "Sedgie Lee" (*Vacation*

Exercise, 92, 97); "sullen Mole" (*WF,* 347) and *Vacation Exercise,* 95. Also, reminiscences of *Il Penseroso* in the poet-meditator's search in *Windsor-Forest* for "sequester'd Scenes" and "Bow'ry Mazes" (261–62). The important point that *Windsor-Forest* assimilates the Edenic elements to postlapsarian conditions through a displacement of Milton's Edenic myth is made persuasively by Sanford Budick in *Poetry of Civilization: Mythopoeic Displacement in the Verse of Milton, Dryden, Pope, and Johnson* (New Haven, 1974), pp. 119–24.

40. Williams, "The 'Fall' of China and *The Rape of the Lock*"; Wasserman, "The Limits of Allusion in *The Rape of the Lock*"; Cleanth Brooks, "The Case of Miss Arabella Fermor," in his *Well Wrought Urn* (New York, 1947), pp. 80–104; and Hugo Reichard, "The Love Affair in Pope's *Rape of the Lock,*" *PMLA* LXIX (1954), 887–902.

41. *PL* IX, 865–66, 874–77; *Rape of the Lock,* I, 121–48; III, 46.

42. *PL* VI, 329–30, and *Rape of the Lock* III, 152; *PL* X, 17–37, and *Rape of the Lock* III, 143–46; *PL* I, 423–24, and *Rape of the Lock* I, 70; *Rape of the Lock* II, 73–74, and *PL* V, 600–01, 702.

43. *Rape of the Lock* V, 9–34; cf. *Iliad* XII, 371–96, and *PL* XII, 575–87.

44. *Dunciad* (1728) I, 1–2. See the fine exposition of the ways in which the first *Dunciad* parodies the *Aeneid* in Aubrey Williams, *Pope's Dunciad,* pp. 9–59.

45. *Dunciad* (1743), IV, 1, fn. 1 (Twickenham, V, 269). The new focus is explored in Williams, *Pope's Dunciad,* pp. 131–58, and in John E. Sitter, *The Poetry of Pope's Dunciad* (Minneapolis, 1971).

46. Budick, *Poetry of Civilization,* pp. 111–55, argues and perhaps overstates the case for an undercurrent of optimism in the poem.

47. See especially the discussion in Williams, *Pope's Dunciad,* pp. 131–58; Sitter, *The Poetry of Pope's Dunciad,* pp. 6–65; and Brower, *The Poetry of Allusion,* pp. 319–61.

48. *Dunciad* I, 118–19; cf. *PL* II, 933–35.

49. *Dunciad* I, 265–86, and *PL* III, 418–97; *Dunciad* II, 1, and *PL* II, 1.

50. See, for example, *Dunciad* II, 63–64, and *PL* II, 948–50.

51. *PL* XI, 366–67, 414–15; *Dunciad* III, 61–67. Also, *PR* III, 265–IV, 365; *Dunciad* III, 73, 79, 101–02.

52. *Dunciad* IV, 141–42; cf. *PL* I, 392–93.

53. *Dunciad* IV, 212, 204, 244; cf. *PL* II, 302–03.

54. *Dunciad* IV, 427–28; *PL* IV, 462–64.

55. *Dunciad* IV, 477–78; *PL* IV, 180–83.

56. *The Anxiety of Influence: A Theory of Poetry* (New York, 1973).

57. See note to *Iliad* II, 255 (Twickenham, VII, 139–40).

BLAKE'S MILTON:
"TO IMMORTALS, . . . A MIGHTY ANGEL"

Joseph Anthony Wittreich, Jr.

> The time is arriv'd when Men shall again converse in Heaven
> & walk with Angels.
>   I am the companion of angels.
>
> —William Blake

MILTONISTS ALL know that Pope disliked Milton's God for being a "school divine"; and most of them presume that Blake liked Milton's Satan, and Milton too—to the extent that he could be numbered among "the Devils party." What they forget (or what perhaps they do not know) is that Thomas Butts, Blake's friend and patron, visited the poet's home, walked into his garden, and found there Blake and his wife, both nude, reading aloud not Books I and II of *Paradise Lost* but Book IV. The poet so widely known for his criticism of Milton in *The Marriage of Heaven and Hell* should also be remembered as the poet who, attentive not to the Satanic but to the visionary books of *Paradise Lost,* wrote an epic to which Milton gave his name. That epic is both a criticism and a celebration. The poem itself points to those moments in Milton's life and art where Blake saw (as he had seen in Wordsworth) "the Natural Man rising up against the Spiritual Man." In such moments, Milton, like Wordsworth, is "No Poet" but "a Heathen Philosopher at Enmity against all true Poetry or Inspiration" (p. 654).[1] In the illuminations accompanying Blake's poem, however, Milton is shown undertaking a journey (see figure 1), encountering his selfhood (see figure 2)—this journey, this encounter, enabling the Spiritual Man to triumph over the Natural Man. In that moment of victory, Milton becomes like Jesus, all Vision, all Imagination (see figure 3).

The first poem, and still the only one, in which one poet elevates another to the rank of epic hero, Blake's *Milton* records the poet's struggle and his triumph—a struggle that involved Milton for most of his life and a triumph that occurred when he set

Figure 1. Plate 1 of Blake's *Milton*, Copy D. Lessing J. Rosenwald Collection, The Library of Congress.

Figure 2. Plate 18 of Blake's *Milton*, Copy D. Lessing J. Rosenwald Collection, The Library of Congress.

Figure 3. Plate 16 of Blake's *Milton*, Copy D. Lessing J. Rosenwald Collection, The Library of Congress.

down the vision of *Paradise Regained*. In this poem, having developed a refined sense of mental revolution, Milton embraces a radical theology. This pattern of development Blake extrapolates from Milton's life and art, mythologizing it into a story in which Milton, having wandered through eternity for a hundred years, determines to descend into the world of generation, in this moment of decision casting off his errors: the doctrine of chastity that disfigured the vision of *Comus*, the politics of violence that scarred the prose works, and the dark cloud of religion that hovered oppressively over the vision of *Paradise Lost*. Annihilating these errors, Milton joins first with his female counterpart Ololon and thereupon with Blake, energizing his successor and, with him, leading the way into Jerusalem. Without a precursor—*without Milton*—Blake's own epic vision would have had no vehicle.

I

All the prophets prophesied by virtue of some influence raying
forth from the spirit of some other prophet into them.
—John Smith

Milton is, for Blake, the model of the true prophet; and the Revelation of Saint John the Divine, the culmination of scriptural prophecy, is a model for his art. These two sources contribute to the poem called *Milton*, the poet providing the poem with its heroic substance and the Bible supplying it with a design, both structural and iconographic. Appropriately, a poem portraying the apotheosis of Milton takes as its context Revelation, which depicts "the Apotheosis of Christ."[2] Without Milton the poem would lack a hero; and without Revelation, Blake's idea of Milton would be, at best, amorphously defined.

Blake accomplishes Milton's elevation to the rank of epic hero by identifying him with various angels of St. John's Apocalypse. In the process, he subscribes to the prophetic tradition of Joachim of Fiore which, acknowledging three ages of the world, finds each of them governed by a prophet who descends to mankind from heaven. Moses presides over the first age and Elijah over the second. The last age has its angel-prophet too, who is identified with various historical figures by commentators on Revelation, and with Milton by Blake. This tradition, to which Blake's poem is firmly tied, receives important modification in the hands of Joachim's successors, and that modification works to the same end as Blake's poem. Joachim's successors made Christ the transitional figure between the first and second ages; and correspondingly, two historical figures in whom Christ will manifest himself will make the transition from the second into the third age, presiding over it as Christ did over the second. One of those figures Blake identifies as Milton, and the other he associates with himself. It is Milton's role, however, that concerns Blake most; and his function in the renovative process is best explained in terms of an analogy developed between the poet and various angels of the Apocalypse. According to a long tradition of commentary on Revelation, the apocalyptic angels are all reproved by St. John for one fault or another; yet even as their vices are condemned their virtues are commended.[3] Whatever their failings, these angels, figured as stars, "give light unto men"; held in Christ's hand, they share in his glory, but they also bring other men into that glory.

Milton, from Blake's point of view, is like the apocalyptic angels, three of them in particular: he falls into error like the third and fifth angels but, upon his transfiguration, resembles the Mighty Angel who instigates the building of Jerusalem. Believing that empire follows art and that poets are the architects of a renovated society, Blake subscribes to the tradition of commentary on Revelation that conceives of Jerusalem not outside, but within history; and he thus conceives of Milton as a *renovator mundi*—a view of him that is pictorialized in four plates associating Milton with angels of the Apocalypse (see figures 1–4) and that is confirmed by four others portraying Milton, emblematically, as a falling star (see, for example, figure 5). Doubly significant, these emblematic portrayals, even as they focus the apocalyptic thrust of Blake's designs, capture their ambiguity, alluding simultaneously to Prometheus, who brought fire down from heaven, thereby enlightening the human race, and to the falling Lucifer, who is regarded by interpreters of Revelation as representative of any one of the great religious heretics or as an emblem for all of them collectively. The star trailing light as a comet conveys both Blake's tribute to Milton and his criticism of him.

The importance of plate 32 (figure 5) to the underlying conception for Blake's poem is suggested by the fact that Blake here magnifies the interlinear design of plate 17 into a full-page illumination for his poem. Both plates, emblematizing Milton as a star, symbolizing through him the light of conversion and of deliverance, carry an allusion to Acts—to the stories of both Saul's conversion and Peter's deliverance. The story of Saul, however, is probably not, as David Erdman argues,[4] the primary referent of

Figure 4. Plate 42 of Blake's *Milton*, Copy D. Lessing J. Rosenwald Collection,
The Library of Congress.

Figure 5. Plate 32 of Blake's *Milton*, Copy D. Lessing J. Rosenwald Collection, The Library of Congress.

Blake's star image; but that story, in its following aspects, is at least incidentally relevant to Blake's poem. First of all, Saul (who is known after his conversion as Paul) goes forth with Barnabas to witness for Christ, and there is eventually sharp contention between the two prophets. This story thus provides a New Testament example of the pairing of prophets and a precedent, too, for the contention that may exist between two prophets as they accept their respective callings. Second, an episode in Paul's life explains the detail of Milton's bald head in plate 18 (figure 2) and, simultaneously, reinforces the thematic content of that plate. In Acts, the shearing of hair is part of the purification rite that Paul undergoes as he is about to enter Jerusalem where he dies for Jesus—dies metaphorically, that is, just as Milton does in plate 18 of Blake's poem (see Acts xii, 25; xv, 39; xviii, 18; xxi, 13, 24).

Yet, even as Blake invites, through these details, recollection of Saul's story, he subordinates that story to that of St. Peter's deliverance, for this episode provides a biblical analogue more in keeping with the accents of Blake's poem. *Milton* is not, as the analogy with Paul would suggest, an account of Blake's conversion. Rather, it recounts Milton's conversion, which makes possible Blake's, and subsequently mankind's, deliverance. Accordingly, the allusion to Paul's conversion becomes an analogue for Milton's experience within Blake's poem: like his biblical prototype, Blake's hero, while under the power of his specter, may be said to have "made havock of the church" (Acts viii, 3); and, like Paul—at times overly zealous of Christian orthodoxy—Milton stretched its dark cloud over England. Such a criticism may be leveled against the Milton of *Comus* and *Paradise Lost*, from Blake's point of view, but not against the Milton of *Paradise Regained*. This Milton, like Paul after his conversion, preaches against blood sacrifice and, adopting an aesthetic of testimony, witnessing to the doctrine of the Resurrection, proceeds to open the eyes of his countrymen (see Acts xiii, 50; xxvi, 13–18). This is also the Milton whom Blake acknowledges to be the agent in his own deliverance; he is the bright light that, shining upon Blake during the Felpham years, releases him from Hayley's prison, just as a comparable light descended upon St. Peter as he lay in prison, chained and sleeping. Paul, then, analogizes Milton's situation, and Peter analogizes Blake's. Like his prototype, Blake falls into a death sleep, becoming "a slave bound in a mill" (p. 703); but also like his prototype, Blake triumphs over the "spectrous Fiend" (p. 702), emerging from his experience with a renewed capacity for vision. Unsurprisingly, then, in their moments of deliverance, Peter and Blake act identically: each prophet, rising out of his death sleep, binds on his sandals and enters the city's gates; thereupon, like Los in plate 1 of *Jerusalem*, each prophet finds a door that he opens and enters, the door signifying Christ, the Crucifixion, the state of self-annihilation. Entering the door which is Christ and the state of self-annihilation that he signifies, each prophet steps into the divine vision, becoming infused with the breath and finer spirit of true prophecy.

Noteworthy, too, is the fact that Peter accomplishes the healing of a man named Aeneas: through Jesus, he "maketh [him] whole" (Acts ix, 33–34). Blake, of course, has been said to perform the same kind of healing operation on his epic hero, Milton. Yet it is probably because Blake wished to discourage such a reading that he subordinated the Peter analogy to those, already pointed to, which are drawn from Revelation. In the process, Blake challenges the view that Milton recanted his precursor's errors rather than his own. Through the fiction of his poem, Blake has Milton recant errors that the poet recognized and cast off during his own lifetime; and in accordance with the pattern established by various angels of John's Apocalypse, Milton is thus shown journeying within and there discovering and divesting himself of those errors which disfigured his vision. Since the primary referents of the star image in plate 32 (figure 5) are to be found in Revelation and because this plate, along with plates 1 and 16 (see figures 1 and 3), is so dependent upon an iconography deriving from the Apocalypse, we should now pursue, in greater detail, the debt that Blake owes to John of Patmos for his Milton designs.

Revelation provides three sources for Blake's star image. There is, first of all, the third angel of the Apocalypse, the star called Wormwood, who focuses the negative meaning in Blake's image. This star, falling from heaven, "burning as it were a lamp," signifies man's falling away from true religion; and it is called Wormwood because it is known by its effects, by the "pestilent institutions" it creates through the perversities of its doctrines.[5] This star, according to Emanuel Swedenborg's commentary on Revelation, symbolizes "all those who are in the love of self" and who thus "falsify the Word."[6] Blake develops this association to suggest that Milton has clouded the divine vision with errors deriving from the selfhood that, in this poem, Milton is poised to destroy (see figure 2).

But in Revelation there are two other stars that emphasize

the positive elements in Blake's image. The fifth angel of the Apocalypse, the Angel of the Bottomless Pit, also appears as a falling star; and the Mighty Angel of chapter 10 is referred to as the Morning Star. In the first instance, the star again signifies the divine vision that is perverted by those who fall away from it. But now the meaning of the image is complicated, for the star is identified with an angel who is about to explore and expose a universe of error. One commentator calls this angel who descends into the pit Reason, who is said to release all those errors which are reason's perversities, errors manifesting themselves in the shape of a beast that the angel then subdues.[7] Swedenborg specifically identifies these errors with "dense falsities . . . originating in the evils of earthly and corporeal loves."[8] Within this context, Blake, by appropriating the star image, chastises Milton for his cruelties to both his wives and daughters. Yet, as Swedenborg explains, the pit this angel is entering—a place of fire, throwing off clouds of smoke—is entered voluntarily; and it has its reference points not in the external world but in "the interiors of the mind," the world within that is being opened, that is ready to be explored.[9] The very act of entering this universe of error, because it is undertaken willingly, promises the exposure of falsities; and this exposure culminates in their annihilation. Like the Angel of the Bottomless Pit, Milton descends into error in order to confront and consolidate it, in order then to cast it off. When Milton completes this act, his prototype changes; Blake identifies him with the Mighty Angel, the Morning Star, the source of true light and of John's divine vision, who is described as an "angel come down from heaven," clothed with a cloud, and having a face that blazes "as it were the sun." This angel, says St. John, "set his right foot upon the sea, and *his* left *foot* on the earth . . . and lifted up his hand to heaven" (x, 1–2, 5).[10] These three angels, then, all of them emblematized as stars, stand behind Blake's portrayals of Milton.

Within Revelation, there are various apocalyptic angels whom some commentators would distinguish, but whom some would identify with one another. Blake, in his protrayals of Milton, holds these two traditions of commentary in dynamic tension. Both the third and fifth angels, commonly understood to be the source of innumerable errors who effect the decay of religion, contrast with the Mighty Angel who is Christ. The contrast is observed by Blake, who allows these different angels to impinge upon his portrayals of Milton. In their associations with Milton, the third and fifth angels epitomize the poet's intellectual faults, and the Mighty Angel serves as a measure of what, by annihilating his errors, Milton becomes. With the coming of the Mighty Angel, "prophecy is restored" as Satan, the Angel of the Bottomless Pit, the enemy within, is overthrown.[11] This triumph is the subject of plate 18 of Blake's *Milton* (figure 2), which draws upon the common understanding that the Mighty Angel of the Apocalypse is Satan's binder.

Yet Blake, apparently cognizant of the other tradition of commentary, blurs this contrast between the Mighty Angel and the other angels of the Apocalypse, observing the idea that all these angels are finally one and the same, distinguished from one another only to define the process whereby errors are purged and renovation accomplished. In plate 1 (figure 1), two images are superimposed, the figure itself recalling, through gesture, the Mighty Angel of the Apocalypse, and the iconography of the design recalling the pit into which the fifth angel of the Apocalypse descends. In this plate, we see Milton, with one foot firmly planted, the other about to enter the sea of time and space, as he lifts up his hand to heaven, dispelling the "erroneous doctrine" that hides his glory and majesty.[12] The errors signified by the clouds are twofold, pointing on the one hand to the sterilities of vision that Milton in his own lifetime overcame and on the other to the disfigurations of his vision caused by obfuscating commentaries of the eighteenth century—commentaries committed, for the most part, to deradicalizing Milton's vision by harnessing it to orthodoxy. Yet it is also in plate 1 that the equation between Milton and the Angel of the Bottomless Pit is made explicit. The flames of fire, the billows of smoke, remind us that when this angel entered the world within "there arose a smoke . . . as the smoke of a great furnace" (ix, 2), the smoke signifying the intellectual failings of those who have perverted the divine vision, as well as the evils that derive from the pride of selfhood and one's attendant failings in earthly love. The effect of the rising smoke is to darken the air and the sun, isolating the erring figure from the divine vision.[13] However, by entering the pit, the figure indicates an awareness of his failings and a desire to effect his regeneration by exposing himself to the fires of purgation.

Blake's *Milton* is the story of a poet's journey, of his pilgrimage; and therefore both plates 1 and 16 depict Milton as a mental traveler. If Revelation's commentators provide one gloss on the clouds in plate 1, Blake provides another, explaining that "those

who are in Eternity" appear in clouds "when any thing of Creation Redemption or Judgment are the Subjects of Contemplation." Moreover, says Blake, the reason they so appear is that they
are in the act of "Humiliating . . . Selfhood & . . . Giving up all to
Inspiration" (p. 553). *Giving up all to inspiration*—that is just
what the Milton of *Paradise Lost* would do. There he represents
himself as surrounded by clouds that, through the agency of celes-
tial light, will be "Purge[d] and disperse[d]" (III, 45–46, 51–54).
In plate 1, as elsewhere then, Blake portrays Milton as Milton
portrayed himself; thus, pushing aside the billowing clouds, Milton is enveloped by purifying flames that enable him both to don
white raiment and to shine like a sun. Having begun his prayer
that introduces the third book of *Paradise Lost* with the hope that
he, like other prophets, would be invested with a mantle, Milton
suggests how he might be portrayed, once his journey is over—a
suggestion that Blake pursues in plate 16. Where Milton is depicted, as is Jesus in Blake's *Vision of the Last Judgment*, "surrounded by Beams of Glory." In his commentary on that painting,
Blake suggests why: in the Divine Humanity, "the Nature of Eternal Things [is] Displayed," all things "beam[ing] from him," because *"as he himself has said All dwells in him"* (pp. 551–52). The
resurrected Milton of plate 16, then, is a type of Christ, the Mighty
Angel and true visionary (see figure 6). And if any line associated
with *Milton* glosses plate 16, it is the one inscribed on the last
plate of Blake's poem—"I return from flames of fire tried & pure &
white"—a line which, closely paraphrasing a verse from the Book
of Daniel ("Many shall be purified, and white, and tried"), includes a promise that those who are purified shall, like Milton,
shine "like the stars" (xii, 3, 10).

In plate 16, Milton shines radiantly, as his black garments are
transformed into white ones unmistakably stained with blood.
This detail reminds us that when Ololon, in the climactic moments of *Milton*, "descended to Felphams Vale / In clouds of
blood, in streams of gore," the Starry Eight, the last of whom is
Milton, "became / One Man Jesus the Saviour" and "round his
limbs / The Clouds of Ololon folded as a Garment dipped in
blood" (42 [49]: 7–8, 11–13). These white garments, rather than
draping Milton's body, are held in his hand, Blake's point being
that the garments, signifying "Christ himself," now cover "the
nakednesse of the soul."[14] To possess them is to have put on
Christ, to be wrapped in his perfection and glory, the white raiment being an emblem of the heroes who through intellectual

Figure 6. Illustration for the Bible: *The Mighty Angel of the Apocalypse.*
The Metropolitan Museum of Art, Rogers Fund, 1914.

warfare release themselves and thereby their civilizations from the powers of darkness. It is therefore fitting that a poem celebrating Milton as a Christian warrior should begin with a lyric poem that celebrates "Mental Fight" (just as Milton did in his two defenses of the English people) as the only form of warfare truly appropriate to man, seeing as its effect the building of Jerusalem in England's green and pleasant land.

A prophet's resemblance to Jesus was said to authenticate him as a prophet; and thus nowhere in the *Milton* designs is the poet more like Jesus than in plate 16 (figure 3), which incorporates, in all its details, the iconography of transfiguration. The clouds of plate 1 have disappeared, the sun rises behind Milton, and a sun circles the poet's head, seeming to radiate from it; Milton's head turned upward, like Christ's both in the vision of the candlesticks and in his appearance as a mighty angel, shows as a sun. In these corresponding moments between Blake's poem and John's prophecy, "the Divine Humanity . . . [is] seen."[15] Christ, who appears in white, with white hair, is the conspicuous reference of plate 16, where Milton, hair streaked with white, holds white raiments in each hand, signifying as they do in the Apocalypse "the divine proceeding, which is divine truth, united with divine goods, which fills the universal heaven, and enters into the interior of the mind." "This," says Swedenborg, "is what is understood by being clothed with white garments."[16] This is a part of the meaning of Blake's design, and its implications are drawn out by Blake himself when he writes, "Naked we come here . . . & naked we shall return. but while clothed with the Divine Mercy" (p. 689).

Another part of Blake's meaning is invested in the image of the sun, its function being to dispel darkness, to enlighten the world, and "to warm and comfort dead . . . bodies, . . . to revive them."[17] Again Blake offers a gloss, this time as he speaks of "Heavenly Men beaming bright" and appearing as "One Man . . . / In . . . beams of gold" (p. 684). Here, in plate 16, not only does the sun radiate upon Milton; but in accordance with Blake's insistence that "Every thing in Eternity shines by its own Internal light" (10 [11]: 16), it radiates from Milton, the suggestion being that one aspect of the poet's struggle involves reception of the divine vision, while another involves its extension. Only in the act of transmitting the vision—making the Word into flesh, hammering it into form—does the poet become the Awakener, and only after his triumph is the apocalyptic moment, involving the renovation of history, able to occur.

II

Joachim [of Fiore] had seen various angels of the Apocalypse as symbols of the new spiritual men. . . . These disciples were brought up into the high mountain and shown both the Promised Land and the crossing of the Jordan which must first be accomplished. Then they saw their own calling: on the one hand, to embody the true spiritual life of the future, and, on the other, to lead the pilgrimage toward the Age of the Spirit. . . . [Thus, through these angels of apocalypse, Joachim] summoned men to . . . spiritual adventure:

Clear the eyes of the mind from all dusts of the earth; leave the tumults of crowds and the clamour of words; follow the angel in spirit into the desert; ascend with the same angel into the great and high mountain; there you will behold high truths hidden from the beginning of time and from all generations. . . . For we, called in these latest times to follow the spirit rather than the letter, ought to obey, going from illumination to illumination, from the first heaven to the second, and from the second to the third, from the place of darkness into the light of the moon, that at last we may come out of the moonlight into the glory of the full Sun.

—Marjorie Reeves

When Blake described his portrayals of Nelson and Pitt in *A Descriptive Catalogue,* he set them within the apotheosis tradition, which he traced to classical antiquity. To this tradition Blake's portrayals of Milton also belong. They are a supreme example of Blake's effort "to emulate the grandeur" of classical and Christian heroes "seen in his vision, and to apply it to modern Heroes" (p. 522); yet once the apotheosis tradition is noted, it should be acknowledged that Blake's portrayals of Milton, though they possess ties with this tradition, involve a radical reassessment of it. Not the first visionary to attempt a portrayal of Milton's apotheosis, Blake, intentionally or not, takes up where one popular rendering of Milton's apotheosis terminated. Once attributed to Dr. Johnson, this earlier rendering, first published in the *Gentleman's Magazine* in 1738, describes the appearance of a figure "girded with white," arm raised, who causes a visionary named William Gutherie to fall to his feet, after which Gutherie, in resistless motion, flies with the figure through air. They come upon a great hall, with a great assembly, on the night Milton is to be admitted to the pantheon of poets; however, what Gutherie witnesses is not Milton's apotheosis but the assembly's denial of it to a poet who is judged defective in character for having been the architect of "black Designs" against the king and state and for having then "varnish[ed] and defend[ed] the most inhuman Action."[18] Blake's *Milton* begins with a judgment of Milton that is no less harsh, scoring him, not for being a revolutionary, but for allowing contradictions in his ideology to impede the revolutionary cause. In plate 1 of *Milton,* the poet walks naked, Blake exposing Milton's faults, so that by overcoming them Milton can be clothed in white (see figures 1 and 3). The apotheosis tradition is thus invoked, but at the same time that Blake observes its literary and artistic conventions he criticizes the philosophy, the morality, that the tradition usually enshrines.

As John Steadman explains, the apotheosis of the hero is a conventional motif whose purpose is to trace a figure's progress toward heroic knowledge, a knowledge that has the status of a divine orthodoxy. The apotheosis tradition, signaled by a flight or by an ascent, depicts a hero, literally or fictively, in a period after his death—a hero who is shown in a region of dark clouds, cleansing himself of error, "of the contagion of earthly sins," and inuring himself "to withstand the pure flames of heaven." This tradition, with its strong apocalyptic overtones, is generally confined "to a handful of verses"; it constitutes "a brief episode" in a long poem.[19] Connections between such a tradition and Blake's poem should be obvious: Blake's *Milton* is about an epiphany that, bringing the poet to illumination, freeing him from his death sleep, causes him to cast off his previous errors.

But besides the parallels between the apotheosis tradition and Blake's poem, there are important deviations from the tradition that are integral to the poem's meaning. The hero's journey is neither a flight nor an ascent; it is a descent into the self and into the world of generation. The apotheosis motif, rather than being relegated to a brief episode, is expanded into the central episode of a brief epic poem. These inversions of tradition point to Blake's reassessment of it, his purpose being to rid a literary and artistic tradition of its usual philosophical underpinnings. Ordinarily the hero's apotheosis is the result of his adopting an attitude of contempt for this world; only by divorcing his soul from his body, only by freeing himself of worldly concerns by taking on the cloak of chastity, is he able to achieve his apotheosis. Blake's point is otherwise. Precisely because Milton exhibited contempt for this world, precisely because he donned the robes of chastity, holding his soul distinct from his body, Milton remained isolated, for most of his life, from the divine vision, from the fiery city of Jerusalem. Milton's errors, then, are the errors of the philosophical tradition

behind the apotheosis motif; and so Milton undertakes his descent
into this world, not a flight from it, which begins with his reenter-
ing his body and which culminates in his union with Ololon, "a
Virgin of twelve years" (36 [40]: 17). This descent finally enables
Milton to achieve an altitude of ascent higher than other poets
because he penetrates and unveils the errors with which other
poets tried to wing their way to Jerusalem.

The pattern of experience represented in Blake's *Milton* is
derived from Milton's own life, a life replete with "signs of pattern" (to use the words of Milton's most recent biographer).[20] The
poet who lost God in his childhood returned to him in old age,
presumably in the act of setting forth the vision of *Paradise Regained.* This observation Blake makes to Henry Crabb Robinson,
but it is also implicit in Blake's reference to Milton's "bright pilgrimage of sixty years" (15 [17]: 52). Milton, born in 1608, had
reached "sixty years" in 1668, the year after *Paradise Lost* was
first published and the year in which he was contemplating, if
not writing, *Paradise Regained.* In his brief epic, Milton breaks
away from the terrifying theology that clouded the vision of his
earlier epic; he returns to the Christocentric theology of his early
poems—a return made possible by an understanding Milton ac-
quired while living and writing under the stress of revolution and,
in a very real sense, experiencing that revolution in his own mind.
Milton thus accomplished his own redemption; and the pattern set
down for it in his own lifetime and preserved in his art became
the pattern by which Blake and his contemporaries could achieve
theirs. In this sense, Milton may be called England's awakener
and redeemer; and in this sense, Milton may be seen within the
lineage of Christ, who created a similar pattern for man's redemption out of his experience in the wilderness.

The primary analogues for Blake's Milton myth are provided,
then, by Milton's own life and by the resemblances Blake observed between it and Christ's experience in the wilderness. Yet
one suspects that Blake perceived yet other analogues that lent
support to the correspondences he had already drawn between
Milton and Christ. His Milton myth, like the Christ myth, involves
a pattern of descent, which may be comprehended metaphorically
(as a descent into the self) but which is portrayed literally (as a
descent into the world of generation). Not only does Christ descend into this world for the Incarnation, but he undertakes another descent, after his death, just before his Resurrection, which
is motivated, as Milton's is, by the desire to rescue Adam *and his*

sons from hell, from their death sleep. The source for Milton's descent can be traced to eighteenth-century poetry and commentary; and the source for Christ's descent is the Gospel of Nicodemus. In each case, the tradition exists in order to accentuate its protagonist's commitment to the human race, his determination to return it to paradise.

These analogues, especially, help to focus (or to refocus) the meaning of Blake's poem. The idea of Milton's returning as England's savior, dramatized in plates 1 and 16, is anticipated by Cowper and Hayley, by Wordsworth and Coleridge. For example, Cowper speaks of Milton as a giant who, now arising from slumber, takes his place among those who are privileged to sleep no more; and Hayley imagines Milton revisiting earth in his mortal character. Wordsworth, in his famous sonnet, cries out: "Milton, thou shouldst be living at this hour / England hath need of thee"; and Coleridge, in a seldom quoted aside, regards Milton as one of the sages and patriots who, though dead, continues to wander through his native country. But this idea of Milton returning to England, which is central to Blake's epic, extends even further back into the eighteenth century than these analogues might suggest. It informs the poetry of Collins and Gray, and the 1738 stage adaptation of *Comus* carries the following prefatory lines:

> *Like some bless'd spirit he* [Milton] *to-night descends,*
> *Mankind he visits, and their steps befriends;*
> *Thro' mazy error's dark perplexing wood,*
> *Points out the path of true and real good.*[21]

These lines, predictably, have not an easy, but an ironic, relationship to the poem Blake has written. They depict "Mankind" wandering "Thro' mazy error's dark perplexing wood," which is where mankind still is when Blake writes his epic, partly because Milton himself is shown, through the fiction of Blake's poem, still lost in error. Thus, it is Milton whom Blake depicts as "a wanderer lost in dreary night" (15 [17]: 16); and it is also Milton who, as a redeemed prophet, finally leads mankind back to the path. Connections of this sort between Milton commentary and Blake's poem proliferate and, in their proliferation, emphasize that the poem called *Milton* is the culmination of a tradition of eighteenth-century criticism that is still too little known, as well as the culmination of a tradition of illustration that depicts "episodes of national history, especially those concerning a struggle for liberty," many of which are "based on scenes from Milton's life." Those

which are, as Marcia Pointon explains, result in "the crystalliza-
tion of the concept of Milton the man as a great revolutionary,
nonconformist protagonist of liberty,"[22] which, current in the early
nineteenth century, is espoused by Blake in his poem.

There is no more evident link between Blake's idea of Milton
and the Milton of the other Romantic poets than their eagerness to
elevate their precursor and themselves into the eschatological position of angels of apocalypse, these angels symbolizing the spiritual
men who will usher in a new order and a new age: like many of
their predecessors, these poets saw their calling as to embody the
spiritual life of the future and to lead the pilgrimage toward it. All
these poets wrote epics, and each of their epics is infused with the
spirit of prophecy whose master theme, whether we are talking
about *Milton* or *Jerusalem*, *The Prelude* or *Prometheus Unbound*, is
the Natural Man becoming the Spiritual Man, his apotheosis being
a prelude to the apotheosis of history. The correlative to the centu-
ries-old tradition of historicizing Antichrist, of seeing him as pope
or high priest, as monarch or ruler, is the historicizing and secularizing of Christ, which involves the belief that he will reign over the
new age in spirit, through the angels of apocalypse, the poets and
prophets who rather than predicting the future help to create it.[23]

III

To be loved for what one is, is the greatest exception. The
great majority love in another only what they lend him, their
own selves, their vision of him.

—Goethe

Blake's portrayals of Milton tell us much about his idea and
about the Romantics' idea of Milton; but they tell us much too
about how all these poets approached Milton: not in an attitude of
contention but in a spirit of collaboration. Yet, recently, a different
story of the Romantics' encounters with Milton has been related.
In *The Anxiety of Influence*, Harold Bloom writes:

*Poetic Influence—when it involves two strong, authentic poets,—always
proceeds by a misreading of the prior poet, an act of creative correction
that is actually and necessarily a misinterpretation. The history of fruitful poetic influence, which is to say the main tradition of Western poetry
since the Renaissance, is a history of anxiety and self-saving caricature,
of distortion, of perverse, wilful revisionism without which modern poetry as such could not exist.*[24]

This proposition is advanced by a critic who, watching Blake
square off against Milton, finds in these two poets a historical

example of the eternal enmity that exists between God and Satan in *Paradise Lost.*

Such a theory of poetic influence is mounted upon a misunderstanding of the Blake-Milton relationship—a relationship that finds its historical models in the involvement of Elisha with Elijah, of Daniel with Jeremiah, and of John of Patmos with Daniel, and that finds its mythic model in *Paradise Lost,* in the relationship of the Father and the Son, the Father shining "Most glorious ... / Substantially express'd," "without cloud / Made visible," in his son (III, 139–40, 385–86). Like the eternal son, the poetic son enables us to behold "visibly" what is there "invisibly" in his poetic father (VI, 681–82); and like the eternal son of *Paradise Regained,* he provides "glimpses of his Father's glory" (I, 93), helping to establish in history what the poetic father decrees. The poetic son, then, manifests the qualities, clarifying and concretizing the vision of his precursor. His objective, his achievement, is not the malforming of his predecessor's vision, but the re-forming of it in such a way that the precursor's vision is released from the malforming operation performed on it by those who did not understand it or by those who, understanding it, did not wish to countenance it.

As the Son relates to his Father in Milton's epics, so Spenser relates to Chaucer and Milton to Spenser. That Blake imagined himself relating to Milton in a similar fashion finds confirmation in Bloom's contention that the opposing aspects of poetic influence may be emblematized by the negative image of "the flowing in of an occult power exercised by humans ... upon humans" or by the positive image of "stars [operating] upon humans."[25] Given these terms, it is noteworthy that when Blake chooses in *Milton* to verbalize, even to pictorialize, his relationship with his hero, he chooses the image of a star (see, for example, figure 5), fully conscious of one commonplace of prophetic literature: "Stars are ministers not masters";[26] rather than darkening the prophet's vision they cast light upon it. The proof text is found in Revelation, where Christ appears as the Morning Star because, according to one student of prophecy, "he illuminates mens wills and understandings," he gives to men "perfect illumination and lightning."[27] Blake's point is that Christ revived revelation rather than caused its cessation, and the last poet to possess it was Milton; hence Blake's willingness to subject himself to Milton's influence in full sympathy with the prophetic dictum that the precursor, even if sometimes mistaken, is not an oppressor but a liberator, that, as the popular expositor of prophetic literature, John Smith, puts it, "under the beams of the greater," the prophet submits to his "irradiations and influence."[28]

Blake's commitment to such a view of poetic influence is openly stated in the poem *Milton*, where the Seven Angels of the Presence weep over Milton's shadow and then, as the Seven Eyes of God, enter the poet's sleeping body, causing Milton to arise and walk with them through Eden "as an Eighth Image Divine" (14 [15]: 42–15 [17]: 1–7; see also 20: 14). Milton, by the end of the poem, is therefore designated as one of "The Eight Immortal Starry-Ones" (34: 4) and, with the other seven, becomes "One Man Jesus the Saviour" (42 [49]: 10–11). The seven angels, the seven spirits, the seven eyes of God—all this imagery finds its source in Revelation. There the seven eyes, referring both to the seven epistles and the seven angels, relate to the cleansing process whereby the doors of perception are successively opened. Appropriating this imagery and then elaborating upon it, Blake represents Milton as the eighth eye, signifying through him the final stage of human consciousness and thereby making him into "a direct emblem of apocalypse."[29] This complex of images, S. Foster Damon once observed, represents "the whole course of human thought in its search for an ideal."[30] For Blake, that search culminates in the poetry of Milton: Milton is the last in a line of prophets before Blake and symbolizes for him the highest peak of imaginative development. In Blake's epic, Milton is repeatedly portrayed out of the same impulse that led Blake to depict Moses and Abraham in *The Vision of the Last Judgment*. As Blake explains in his lengthy commentary on that painting, these biblical figures are to be understood as "the States Signified by . . . [their] Names, the Individuals being representatives or Visions of those States" (p. 546). Since man, through Milton, passes from the seventh eye of Jesus to the eighth eye of his Second Coming, Milton epitomizes, for Blake, the "inward-turning" process that culminates in apocalypse, in the highest state of mental freedom which is finally no state but human existence itself.[31] The seven eyes, the seven spirits, the seven angels of John's Apocalypse were traditionally associated with Christ's ministers who are charged with the building up of Jerusalem. By adding Milton to this assemblage, Blake makes clear that Milton is the city's master-builder, crediting his precursor with being the last, the most capacious, and thus, potentially, the most effectual of the apocalyptic angels.

Revelation, then, provides Blake with a precedent for his

eighth apocalyptic angel and, so doing, enables Milton to enter into the same relationship with Blake that Revelation's eighth angel enjoys with John of Patmos. Of that angel we are told that "the earth was lightened with his glory" and that, upon proclaiming himself as John's fellow prophet, the two together give "the testimony of Jesus" (xviii, 1; xix, 10). The figure of the eighth angel, through his relationship with John, is thus irrevocably linked to the story of the "two Witnesses"—a story that provides still further insight into Blake's alliance with Milton, yielding a biblical model for it.

St. John's account of the two witnesses is invoked in Blake's *Milton* by references to two sets of historical types—Whitefield and Wesley, Milton and Blake—and is accompanied by the suggestion that their prototype is the Bard ("Let the Bard himself *witness*," Blake says in plate 13). Even more directly, the story is the undoubted reference of the inscription Blake writes on the final plate of his poem: "I return from flames of fire tried & pure & white." That inscription has been explained as a cryptic reference to the conclusion of Milton's *Comus*, a poem Blake was illustrating as he was conceiving, if not writing, his own poem.[32] But, more to the point, Blake's inscription, as we have already observed, is a near quotation of a passage from the Book of Daniel, a passage often recalled marginally in exegesis of the story of John's two witnesses. Belonging to the last age and generally thought to be two particular men, the witnesses had been identified with various historical personages. Blake identifies them with Milton and himself, his point being that it is not the priests of the church but the poet-prophets who are the fullest approximations of these biblical models. To know who the witnesses are and what they represent is to understand more fully Blake's idea of Milton, as well as his idea of himself in relation to Milton. Their story, as told by St. John, epitomizes the meaning of Blake's poem and, at the same time, confirms the meaning we have already assigned to the iconography of plates 1 and 16.

The two witnesses of Revelation, dying and reviving after three and one-half days (that is, years), are called "two prophets" because they bear witness to the truth of a new life. These witnesses, as Henry More explains, are not naturally dead; instead John's reference is to "their Moral and Political Life and Resurrection"—they are *"alive,* or *slain,* either in a *Political,* or *Moral* sense." No sooner do the two witnesses "begin to perform their office of witnessing to the truth," says More, than they are "assaulted, suppressed, kept out of power, and *politically* killed"; but just as their death is political so too is their resurrection.[33] Their rising is a prelude to apocalypse, with England providing the stage on which it can be enacted.

The witnesses in Revelation recall all the famous pairs of prophets in the Old Testament: Moses and Aaron, Elijah and Elisha, Zerubbabel and Joshua. Builders of Jerusalem, they are charged with measuring, constructing, and finishing the temple; and their authenticity is established by their apparel, by their exchanging filthy garments for white ones. It was understood by commentators on Revelation such as Joseph Mede and also Samuel Hartlib (Milton's friend who helped to popularize Mede's commentary) that white garments stained with blood are evidence that a hero, having undergone Christ's sacrifice (metaphorically through the annihilation of selfhood), has been redeemed by it.[34]

The changing of the garments thus occurs in a moment of symbolic death. Christ may have been crucified literally; but Milton and Blake, conforming to his pattern, are crucified metaphorically—Milton by succumbing to the politics of violence through his defense of regicide and Blake by acquiescing in the politics of withdrawal through his retreat to Felpham. In this sense, both poets are self-crucified, but they are both politically crucified as well, by a society that would distort, confuse, and even suppress their respective visions. Each poet dies, then, but each is also resurrected, both in his own lifetime and in his successors. In his own lifetime, Milton rises up, most notably, with the publication of *Paradise Regained;* and in his lifetime, Blake rises up on two occasions: first, when having fallen into a three-day death sleep following his brother's death, he awakened from it into the divine vision[35]; and later, when returning to London, after his three and one-half years' stay in Felpham, he renewed his commitment to visionary art. (In *Milton,* quite evidently, Blake mythologizes not only experiences from Milton's life but experiences from his own, an understanding that goes a long way toward explaining why, besides the eleven portrayals of Milton, there are portrayals of both Blake and his brother.) Both poets are also resurrected in their successors: Milton rising up in Blake and the other romantic poets, and Blake rising up in various modern poets who, like Yeats, set out to define his system just as Blake attempted to lay open Milton's. In this respect, both poets are like Elijah, who was said to rise up in John the Baptist, who, in turn, seemed to rise up again in Christ. In each instance, the rising witnesses represent a "great turn of things," a "hastening to the New Jerusalem," and their subsequent ascents into heaven are translated into a symbol both of their apotheosis and of the apotheosis of history they are expected to accomplish.[36] As mankind's deliverers from tyranny and servitude, the two witnesses, Milton and Blake, "pull downe errours and wicked vices."[37] They are revolutionaries who, like Christ, "confoundeth all traditions, and subverteth all constitutions,"[38] and whose story Blake invokes, believing with various commentators on Revelation that "God stirs up many of the English spirits . . . to finish what was before left incomplete."[39] And Blake appears to be committed, with these same commentators, to the idea that those who "receiveth a Prophet in the name of a Prophet shall receive a Prophet's reward."[40] So it is that Blake receives Milton and that he invites us to receive not just Milton but also himself.

In his portrayals of Milton, Blake remembers that the prophet's reward is a halo, which, shining like the sun, symbolizes his transcendent glory and special office; that the prophet, though called a star, is not just any star but the brightest in the firmament. According to Joseph Mede, the fallen prophet rolls great clouds through the heavens; yet fallen prophets rise again, and we know when their resurrection commences for they appear as stars breaking through the clouds, and we know, too, when their resurrection is completed for then they appear as the sun, signifying that the Word eventually pierces the dark cover that would conceal it.[41] Milton's resurrection begins in plate 1 (figure 1) of Blake's poem: this is made clear by the fact that at exactly the point where Milton's hand rolls back the clouds (in the upper right-hand corner), a star shoots forth on the next plate; and Milton's resurrection is completed in plate 16 (see figure 3), where the poet, holding white garments in both hands, has his head encircled by a sun.

Blake's *Milton,* then, rather than corroborating a theory of poetic influence predicated upon "anxiety," serves as a check upon it. And a similar check may be found outside this poem, in a response Blake makes to one of Lavater's aphorisms—a response that shows Blake standing in defiance of those who believe with Harold Bloom that St. Paul's admonition, "let each esteem others better than themselves," delineates "a pattern that no poet whatever could bear to emulate."[42] When Lavater writes, *"Who seeks those that* are greater *than himself, their greatness* enjoys, *and forgets his greatest* qualities *in their greater ones, is* already *truly great,"* Blake responds, "I hope I do not flatter my self that this is pleasant to me" (p. 577). The notion that Blake suffered under the anxiety of influence, that he was obsessed by a drive to transcend Milton, even at the cost of misrepresenting and misinterpreting him, is antithetical not only to the spirit of Blake's rejoinder to Lavater but to the principle of art that Blake enunciates in *A Descriptive Catalogue:* "To suppose that Art can go beyond the finest specimens of Art that are now in the world," says Blake, "is not knowing what Art is; it is being blind to the gifts of the spirit"—a principle, let it be noted, that follows upon Blake's remark that Milton represents "the extent of the human mind" (p. 535). Indeed, Harold Bloom's theory of influence negates the message that Blake allows to climax first *The Marriage of Heaven and Hell* ("The worship of God is. Honouring his gifts in other men each according to his genius, and loving the greatest men best" [plates 22–23]) and then *Jerusalem,* where in almost identical words he appeals, "Go, tell them that the Worship of God, is honouring his gifts / In other men: & loving the greatest men best, each according / To his Genius" (91: 7–9).

Blake, his own words testify, was not psychologically crippled by Milton; rather, he admits to having had the joy of seeing the divine countenance more distinctly in him than in any other hero. The donning of the bright sandal in Blake's *Milton* occurs at a crucial moment—the moment of union between Blake and Milton. It should be understood in terms of the convention of prophecy which, recognizing that walking without sandals is a sign of great poverty or deep mourning, asserts that, conversely, strapping on the sandal signifies that the prophet, no longer impoverished, has achieved an integrated personality, is about to throw his entire being into his prophecy, making not his lips only, but his whole personality, the vehicle for the divine Word. Milton, in the full possession of all his prophetic faculties, is the ideal that Blake aspires to become, that he does become in this moment of union. In this moment, Blake does what Dante would not do.

Dante had taken Virgil as his guide in the *Commedia;* by taking Milton as his own guide in *Milton,* Blake introduces an analogy only to violate it. As a guide, Virgil was abandoned at the moment when Dante came to the threshold of paradise. In contrast, it is at exactly the moment when Blake is ready to enter eternity that Milton joins him: grasping Milton, in the form of "a bright sandal," becoming energized by him, Blake is now ready to walk with his mentor "forward thro' Eternity." The contrasting status that Blake here assigns to Dante and Milton is underscored by the eagle that figures so prominently in both the *Commedia* and Blake's *Milton*. In the *Commedia*, the eagle awakens Dante; but in Blake's epic, the eagle *as Milton*[43] is poised to awaken Albion, to ready England for Apocalypse (see figure 4). This idea, if not this very figure, stands behind most Romantic criticism of Milton.

In their idea of Milton, the Romantics found a motive for their criticism. Milton set out to rescue men from the oppressive orthodoxies of civilization; and the Romantics, in turn, none more notably than Blake, undertook to release Milton from the prisons of critical orthodoxy that had manacled his vision. Unveiling the Miltonic vision, these poets could assist Milton in the task with which they charged him. Their criticism, to be sure, is pointed, yet usually judicious; but it is also orchestrated as a symphony of praise, honoring not Milton alone but the whole tradition of poetry that, because he perfected and popularized it, Milton may be said to have fathered.

The Milton tradition, I should say in conclusion, is what Blake understood it to be, the tradition of prophecy; and that tradition is rich indeed, involving a way of seeing and a way of writing—indeed, a whole system of aesthetics. In addition, prophecy involves a way of relating: it postulates a theory of influence and provides a paradigm for intrapoetic relationships. But a word of caution: prophecy does not explain *all* poetic relationships; and it certainly does not provide, as Harold Bloom attempts to do, a paradigm for all "fruitful poetic influence . . . since the Renaissance."[44] Instead, prophecy sustains a view of poetry, like Shelley's, that emphasizes its interconnectedness, its progressive character—a view of poetry that pertains not to poets who approach their precursors as if they were grab bags to steal from or Nobodaddys they must run away from, but to those who encounter their predecessors in an attitude of cooperation. In *The Arte of Prophecying*, William Perkins makes the point admirably well, observing, in accordance with 1 Corinthians xiv, 31–32, that "Prophets . . . are not to be reprooved of other Prophets," for they "prophesy one by one," each new prophet being "subject to" his predecessors.[45] Prophecy, then, is creation, not *ex nihilo* but out of preexistent matter; accordingly, prophets study old prophecies by way of creating new ones, old prophecy, as one commentator on Revelation puts it, providing "the frame" from which new prophecy "is fetched."[46] Visionary art is thus marked by interdependence, by a "multifarious Allusivenesse"[47] that establishes continuity between prophecies and communion among prophets. Such communion Blake sought with Milton and many moderns have sought with both poets.

The collective influence of Milton and Blake is evident in many quarters, some unexpected. Much has already been said about how modern poets have echoed Milton and Blake—their words, phrases, even their ideas. What needs to be said is that this echoing process, operating in accordance with prophetic tradition, does not imply a paucity of poetic talent. Rather, its purpose is to indicate a relationship, to authenticate it, by confirming old prophecy anew and by throwing new light on its import. This process, because it yokes together the old and the new, also punctuates the interdependence of visionary art. Christopher Wordsworth understood this principle well and, in fact, traced it to Revelation, where, he explains, repeated words and phrases "serve to connect one portion with another," showing that the Apocalypse is interwoven with the prophecies of the Old Testament to form "a compact whole with them."[48] Authenticated by scriptural prophecy, the same process is operative in English poetry, joining the poems of Chaucer, Spenser, and Milton with those of the Romantics and moderns. Their various poems, to appropriate words from Shelley's *Defence of Poetry*, are "episodes to that great poem which all poets, like the cooperating thoughts of one great mind, have built up since the beginning of the world." The lesson in the poetics of influence to be learned from Shelley is the same one that Milton, through his poetry and prose, taught Blake and that Blake, through *Milton*, delivered to future generations of artists—to those, that is, with the eyes to see and the ears to hear.

University of Maryland, College Park

NOTES

Research for this essay was conducted during my tenure as a fellow of the Folger Shakespeare Library, and the essay was written while I held grants from the National Endowment for the Humanities and the University of Wisconsin's Institute for Research in the Humanities.

1. All quotations of Blake, the sources of which are given parenthetically within the text, are from *The Poetry and Prose of William Blake*, rev. ed., ed. David

V. Erdman (New York, 1970). My observations on the illuminations for *Milton* are based upon Copy D of the poem, owned by Lessing J. Rosenwald, which is now in the Library of Congress. Because Erdman does not number full-page designs, his numbering of plates does not correspond with Copy D; I have therefore inserted in brackets the corresponding plate number of Copy D. Thus 15 [17]: 47–48 means plate 15, lines 47–48, in the Erdman edition, which corresponds with plate 17 in Copy D. For a full discussion of the different versions of the plates reproduced with this essay, see my *Angel of Apocalypse: Blake's Idea of Milton* (Madison, Wis., 1975), pp. 13–48. The present essay develops a number of perceptions that are scattered through my book.

2. Henry More, *Apocalypsis Apocalyseos; or the Revelation of St. John the Divine Unveiled* (London, 1680), p. xvii.

3. For the tradition behind Blake's identification, see Marjorie Reeves, *The Influence of Prophecy in the Later Middle Ages: A Study of Joachimism* (Oxford, 1969), pp. 143, 154, but also pp. 193, 209, 232–33, 354, 443; and see also George Gifford, *Sermons upon the Whole Booke of the Revelation* (London, 1599), p. 33.

4. *The Illuminated Blake* (New York, 1974), pp. 217, 248.

5. David Pareus, *A Commentary upon the Divine Revelation of the Apostle and Evangelical John*, tr. Elias Arnold (Amsterdam, 1644), pp. 161–64.

6. *The Apocalypse Explained According to the Spiritual Sense*, 5 vols. (New York, 1846–47), nn. 517–19.

7. Ludowick Muggleton, *A True Interpretation of the Eleventh Chapter of St. John* (1662; rpt. ed., London, 1833), p. 118.

8. *The Apocalypse Explained*, n. 533.

9. Ibid., n. 536.

10. The Mighty Angel of the Apocalypse, because his hand is raised, is customarily associated with the Angel in the Book of Daniel; see, for example, William Fulke, *Praelections upon the Sacred and Holy Revelation of S. John*, tr. George Gifford (London, 1573), p. 64; and Henry Bullinger, *A Hundred Sermons upon the Apocalypse of Jesu Christ* (London, 1573), pp. 130 ff. The contrast between the Angel of the Bottomless Pit and the Mighty Angel of John's Apocalypse is interestingly developed by William Guild, *The Sealed Book Opened* (London, 1656), p. 100: the Mighty Angel comes down with a face like a sun (that is, bringing light with him), whereas the Angel of the Bottomless Pit, enveloped by smoke and clouds, brings darkness; the Mighty Angel is thus charged with dispelling the errors, with rolling back the dark clouds created by his adversary. Blake sees Milton as his own adversary, and thus in plate 1 (figure 1) Milton is shown overcoming (that is, dispersing) the errors of the Natural Man. Blake's conception is in keeping with Guild's belief that Christians "mis-know" Antichrist: "the seduced Christian looks for an individual Antichrist" in history; the true Christian finds the Antichrist within and thereupon extirpates him (sig. A4).

11. See Patrick Forbes, *An Learned Commentarie upon the Revelation of Saint John* (Middleburg, 1614), p. 81.

12. *His glory, his majesty*—these are the qualities, judging from inscriptions that accompany Milton portraiture of the eighteenth century, that artists before Blake attempted to capture in their portrayals of the poet. Many eighteenth-century portraits of Milton carry Dryden's famous epigram, which represents Milton as surpassing both Homer and Virgil in "loftiness of thought" and "Majesty"; another epigram by Jonathan Richardson, Jr., accompanying a portrait by his

father, represents Milton as a "Fierce Dazling light," calling Milton "Another Sun" (the tradition is charted by John Rupert Martin, *The Portrait of Milton at Princeton and Its Place in Milton Iconography* [Princeton, 1961], see esp. plates 7, 8, 11, and 13).

13. These associations are developed by Swedenborg in *The Apocalypse Explained*, n. 533. In *The Influence of Prophecy in the Later Middle Ages*, Reeves provides a useful gloss on the idea behind Blake's title-page design, explaining that "in the development of the Sibylline prophecies we see the desire for a human triumph in history struggling with the conviction that only divine intervention can overcome the inherent evil in man. From this conflict of ideas" (and I would argue that precisely this conflict of ideas stands behind Blake's poem) emerges the figure of a human savior (in Blake's poem, Milton), "a Last Emperor who achieves a partial triumph before the final onset of evil and the final spiritual intervention" (p. 299). That figure, Reeves notes, appears in clouds (see figure 1) at the moment just before his triumph (see figure 3).

14. William Perkins, *Lectures upon the Three First Chapters of the Revelation* (London, 1604), p. 323. Blake here toys with the paradox prominent in commentary on Revelation: that a body clothed conceals a naked soul; that, conversely, a naked body reveals a soul clothed in Christ. It should be noted as well that, while the coloration of the garments in Copy D suggests the blood-stained garments in both Revelation and the final plates of *Milton*, another detail, Milton's foot on the garment, reminds us that the poet is able to assume white garments (to become clothed with Christ and with Ololon) only because, and only after, he casts off his filthy garments. Plate 16 gathers both moments into a single illumination.

15. Swedenborg, *The Apocalypse Explained*, n. 65.

16. Ibid. The rending of the garment in two pieces, as it appears in plate 16 (figure 3), involves an allusion to 2 Kings ii, 12; and the rending occurs at the moment that the mantle of prophecy is passed from Elijah to Elisha—in Blake's poem at the moment it is passed from Milton to Blake. Correspondingly, that moment signals for Milton, as it does for Elijah, his transfiguration, his apotheosis.

17. Perkins, *Lectures*, pp. 105–06.

18. See "The Apotheosis of Milton, A Vision," *Gentleman's Magazine*, VIII (1738), 223–35, 469, 521–22; IX (1739), 20–21, 73–75. John Hawkins included this piece in volume 11 of *The Works of Samuel Johnson* (London, 1787–88). On the attribution, see *Monthly Review*, LXXVII (1787), 69.

19. *Disembodied Laughter: Troilus and the Apotheosis Tradition* (Berkeley and Los Angeles, 1972), pp. 37–38.

20. William Riley Parker, *Milton: A Biography*, 2 vols. (Oxford, 1968), II, 1065.

21. I quote from *Comus: A Masque* (London, 1750), p. 5.

22. *Milton and English Art* (Manchester, 1970), p. xxvii; see also n. 12 of this essay.

23. On the historicizing of Satan, see Christopher Hill, *Antichrist in Seventeenth-Century England* (London, 1971), but also Reeves, *Influence of Prophecy*; on the secularizing of Christ, see M. H. Abrams, *Natural Supernaturalism: Tradition and Revolution in Romantic Literature* (New York, 1971).

24. (New York, 1973), p. 30. Bloom applies his theory, not to Blake, but to a number of other poets including Spenser and Milton, Wordsworth and Shelley, in *A Map of Misreading* (New York, 1975). Here the Spenser-Milton relationship replaces the Milton-Blake relationship of *The Anxiety of Influence*, becoming a new paradigm for the operation of poetic influence. It is noteworthy that in *A Map*

of Misreading Blake is scarcely mentioned, one suspects because he is too much the idealist: "Poets, supposedly defending poetry, idealize their relationship to one another," writes Bloom, "and the magical Idealists among critics follow the poets in this self-deception. Northrop Frye idealizes more powerfully than ever Blake does" (p. 199). Nonetheless, we must conclude, as Bloom seems to do, that Blake does *idealize:* specifically, he idealizes his relationship with Milton in *Milton;* then he writes *Jerusalem* under Milton's sway.

25. *Anxiety of Influence*, p. 39. In *A Map of Misreading*, Bloom observes that "poets tend to think of *themselves* as stars because their deepest desire is to be an influence, rather than to be influenced, but even in the strongest, whose desire is accomplished, the anxiety of having been formed by influence still persists" (pp. 12–13; italics added). In *Milton*, it should be emphasized, Blake depicts Milton, not himself, as a star, thereby celebrating rather than retreating from the poet whose vision helps to shape his own. Analogously, in his famous sonnet, "London, 1802," Wordsworth represents Milton as "a Star" (9): Milton, he says, is "Pure as the naked heavens, majestic, free" (11). *Pure*, one supposes, and *free* from the anxieties that Bloom ascribes to him and to his Romantic successors.

26. William Lilly, *Merlinus Anglicus Junior: The English Merlin Reviv'd*, 2d ed. (London, 1644), sig. [A1ʳ].

27. Perkins, *Lectures*, p. 250.

28. "Of Prophecy," in *A Collection of Theological Tracts*, ed. Richard Watson, 6 vols. (London, 1785), IV, 362.

29. Harold Bloom, *Blake's Apocalypse: A Study in Poetic Argument* (New York, 1963), p. 441.

30. *A Blake Dictionary: The Ideas and Symbols of William Blake* (Providence, R.I, 1965), p. 134.

31. See Andrew Wright, *Blake's Job: A Commentary* (Oxford, 1972), p. 3; and for what is still the finest exposition of this symbolism as it is used by Blake, see also Northrop Frye, *Fearful Symmetry: A Study of William Blake* (1947; rpt. ed., Boston, 1962), esp. pp. 360–61 and 448–49.

32. See Irene Tayler, "Say First! What Mov'd Blake? Blake's *Comus* Designs and *Milton*," in *Blake's Sublime Allegory: Essays on The Four Zoas, Milton, and Jerusalem*, ed. Stuart Curran and Joseph Anthony Wittreich, Jr. (Madison, Wis., 1973), p. 257. The position that the inscription has no real bearing on this design has been taken, most recently, by John E. Grant in an essay that comments helpfully on designs not attended to in my own essay. See "The Female Awakening at the End of Blake's *Milton:* A Picture Story, with Questions," in *Milton Reconsidered: Essays in Honor of Arthur E. Barker*, ed. John Karl Franson (Salzburg, 1976), pp. 95, 97.

33. *Apocalypsis Apocalypseos*, pp. 105–08; and see also Thomas Goodwin, *An Exposition of the Revelation* (1639), in *The Works of Thomas Goodwin*, 12 vols. (Edinburgh, 1861–66), III, 158–59, 189, 190–91.

34. See Mede's *Key of the Revelation*, tr. Richard More, 2d ed. (London, 1650), p. 112; and Hartlib et al., *The Revelation Reveled by Two Apocalyptical Treatises* (London, 1651), pp. 57, 67.

35. See Kaethe Wolf-Gumpold, *William Blake: Painter, Poet, Visionary*, tr. Ernest Rathgeben (London, 1969), p. 26.

36. Goodwin, *Exposition*, in *Works*, III, 149, 182, 192; see also Mede, *Key of the Revelation*, p. 23.

37. Gifford, *Sermons*, p. 197.

38. Bullinger, *A Hundred Sermons*, p. 46.

39. See, for example, Mede, *Key of the Revelation*, p. 110.

40. Ibid.

41. Discourse XLII," in *The Works of Joseph Mede*, 2 vols. (London, 1664), I, 314–15; and also in *Works*, see "Discourse XXIII," I, 110–13.

42. *Anxiety of Influence*, p. 91.

43. The eagle, it should be noted, is a component of the iconography that develops around Milton portraiture in the eighteenth century.

44. *Anxiety of Influence*, p. 30.

45. In *The Works of Mr. W. Perkins*, 3 vols. (Cambridge, 1613), II, 664.

46. Richard Bernard, *A Key of Knowledge for the Opening of the Secret Mysteries of St. Johns Mysticall Revelation* (London, 1617), p. 89.

47. I borrow the phrase from Henry More, *An Exposition of the Seven Epistles to the Seven Churches* (London, 1669), p. 143.

48. *The Apocalypse* (London, 1849), p. xii.

WORDSWORTH ON MILTON
AND THE DEVIL'S PARTY

Edna Newmeyer

O F T H E many controversies—literary, political, and theological—that have erupted over the interpretation of *Paradise Lost,* perhaps the most curious revolves around the concept of Milton's Satan as rebel-hero. First adumbrated by Blake and expatiated in diverse circumstances and connotations by Hazlitt, Byron, and Shelley, this was the preponderant view of Milton's Satan held by writers, critics, and presumably readers throughout the nineteenth century. There were a few dissenters, of course. Calvin Huckaby credits Walter Savage Landor and John Wilson with being the first nineteenth-century critics to see the error of regarding Satan as the hero of *Paradise Lost;*[1] Benjamin T. Sankey claims the distinction for Coleridge, whose view of Milton's Satan as the prototype of tyranny and evil was made public as early as 1809.[2] Neither makes mention of Wordsworth's position in the controversy, nor does James G. Nelson in discussing the origins of the idea of Satan as Faustian hero.[3]

There has been little or no comment on what "the Best Knower of Milton"[4] thought of Milton's Satan. And there is an even more remarkable paucity of direct and recorded expression on this subject from Wordsworth himself. We have three comments in all, the earliest of which may be his manuscript note in a second-edition copy of *Paradise Lost;*[5] and the other two are reported by Hazlitt (ca. 1800) and by Lady Richardson (1844).[6] Hazlitt relates that "Wordsworth once said that he could read the description of Satan in Milton, . . . [*PL* I, 592–94] till he felt a certain faintness come over his mind from a sense of beauty and grandeur." This observation, in conjunction with his manuscript note, seems to indicate that Wordsworth shared his contemporaries' admiration for Satan's heroic qualities. The note is not directed at the same passage in *Paradise Lost* to which Hazlitt alludes; it is concerned with Milton's description of Satan's punishment following his triumphant return to hell after effecting the fall of Adam and Eve (*PL* X, 504–70). But

83

Wordsworth's criticism of Milton's degradation of Satan is written with the earlier passage in mind:

Here we bid farewell to the first character, perhaps ever exhibited in Poetry. And it is not a little to be lamented that, he leaves us in a situation so <little in> degraded in comparison with the grandeur of his introduction. Milton's fondness for the Metamorphoses probably induced him to draw this picture which <I cannot exc> excellently as it [is] executed I cannot but think unworthy of his genius. The "spattering noise" &c. are images which can <not but> only excite disgust. The representation of the Fallen Angels wreathing [sic] their jaws filled with soot and cinders with hatefullest disrelish contains in it nothing that can afford pleasure. Had the poet <chosen to> determined to inflict upon them a so physical punishment certainly one more noble more consonant to the dignity of the beings might easily [cetera desunt].[7]

On the other hand, Lady Richardson's report of her conversation with Wordsworth toward the end of his life and at the height of the Satanist controversy shows that Wordsworth did not mistake the grandeur and nobility of Milton's conception for an intention, conscious or not, to depict Satan as a hero worthy of our moral sympathy and admiration:

He thought [Dr. Arnold] was mistaken in the philosophy of his view of the danger of Milton's Satan being represented without horns and hoofs; that Milton's conception was as true as it was grand; that making sin ugly was a common-place notion compared with making it beautiful outwardly, and inwardly a hell. It assailed every form of ambition and worldliness, the form in which sin attacks the highest natures.

One might conclude from this ostensible contradiction between his early and later comments that the young Wordsworth regarded Satan as heroic and laudable and that the older Wordsworth, grown religiously and politically conservative, is correcting the rash and radical affinities of his youth. Succeeding evidence will demonstrate, however, that no such contradiction exists. As early as 1796–1797, when Wordsworth wrote *The Borderers*, his concept of Milton's Satan was consistent with his remarks to Lady Richardson. His criticism, in the manuscript note, of the images employed in Milton's punishment of Satan as being "unworthy" of Milton's genius, disgusting, and containing "nothing that can afford pleasure" expressed disapproval of what he considered a breach of poetic decorum and not indignation at unjust treatment of a noble hero.[8] Young or old, Wordsworth did not agree with Blake that Milton was "of the Devil's party without knowing it"; nor did he share Hazlitt's extravagant admiration for Satan as Promethean-Napoleonic hero.[9] He would not have endorsed Byron's sanguine assurance that Satan was the hero of *Paradise Lost.*[10] Nor would he have sanctioned Shelley's inordinate allegations: that Milton asserted "no superiority in moral virtue to his God over his Devil"; that he had done all that could be done to "excite the sympathy . . . of succeeding generations of mankind" for the rebel Satan; and that, having given "the Devil all imaginable advantage," whether "Milton was a Christian or not, at the period of the composition of Paradise Lost," was open to question.[11]

Wordsworth gives us no manifest evaluation of Satan's character, as Coleridge does, but what Coleridge states explicitly provides insight into what Wordsworth says by implication. One of Coleridge's earliest interpretations of Milton's Satan occurs in his attempt to analyze Napoleon's character[12] for the "Letters on the Spaniards" that appeared in the *Courier* (December–January 1809–1810):

It is indispensable, that men should have clear conceptions of what the main power of a remorseless tyrant, such as Bonaparte, consists in. This cannot lie in vice as vice, for all injustice is in itself feebleness and disproportion; but . . . the abandonment of all principle of right enables the soul to choose and act upon a principle of wrong and to subordinate to this one principle all the various vices of human nature. . . . He who has once said with his whole heart, Evil, be thou my good! has removed a world of obstacles by the very decision, that he will have no obstacles but those of force and brute matter.[13]

Coleridge expands these ideas in Appendix C to *The Statesman's Manual* (1816),[14] where he defines Milton's Satan as the paradigm for all "the Masters of Mischief, the Liberticides, and mighty Hunters of Mankind, from NIMROD to NAPOLEON." What marks such natures, he explains, is that the will in "its utmost abstraction and consequent state of reprobation"

becomes satanic pride and rebellious self-idolatry in the relations of the spirit to itself, and remorseless despotism relatively to others; the more hopeless as the more obdurate by its subjugation of sensual impulses, by its superiority to toil and pain and pleasure; in short, by the fearful resolve to find in itself alone the one absolute motive of action, under which all other motives from within and from without must be either subordinated or crushed.

This is the character which Milton has so philosophically as well as sublimely embodied in the Satan of his Paradise Lost.

He deplores how often this character has "been embodied in real life" and has "given a dark and savage grandeur" to history:

> Wherever it has appeared, under whatever circumstances of time and country, the same ingredients have gone to its composition. . . . Hope in which there is no Cheerfulness; Stedfastness within and immovable Resolve, with outward Restlessness and whirling Activity; Violence with Guile; Temerity with Cunning; . . . Interminableness of Object with perfect Indifference of Means.

Hazlitt, in his own essay on Milton, uses this antipathetic characterization of Satan, and of Napoleon, to support his contrary appraisal:

> A noted political writer of the present day has exhausted nearly the whole account of Satan in the Paradise Lost, by applying it to a character whom he considered as after the devil (though I do not know whether he would make even that exception) the greatest enemy of the human race.[15]

In his lectures on Milton in 1818, Coleridge added further refinements to his analysis of Satan. They show that grandeur and sublimity can go along with great evil and that to call Satan sublime is not necessarily to find him praiseworthy or heroic:

> The character of Satan is pride and sensual indulgence, finding in self the sole motive of action. It is the character so often seen *in little* on the political stage. It exhibits all the restlessness, temerity, and cunning which have marked the mighty hunters of mankind from Nimrod to Napoleon. The common fascination of men is, that these great men, as they are called, must act from some great motive. Milton has carefully marked in his Satan the intense selfishness, the alcohol of egotism, which would rather reign in hell than serve in heaven. To place this lust of self in opposition to denial of self or duty, and to show what exertions it would make, and what pains endure to accomplish its end, is Milton's particular object in the character of Satan. But around this character he has thrown a singularity of daring, a grandeur of sufferance, and a ruined splendour, which constitute the very height of poetic sublimity.[16]

What reason have we to assume that Wordsworth held a similar view of Milton's Satan? The Wordsworth and Coleridge letters give ample evidence that this question must have been a matter of almost daily conversation in the years 1808–1809. Coleridge was living with the Wordsworths during this period when Wordsworth was writing *The Convention of Cintra* and Coleridge his *Letters on the Spaniards*. We may even conclude that Coleridge's Spanish *Letters* were a by-product of his involvement in the composition of Wordsworth's pamphlet. Not only was Coleridge instrumental in the publication of extracts from *The Convention* in the *Courier*,[17] but he also claims to have written portions of *The Convention,* even to dictating the substance of De Quincey's explanatory note.[18] While composing the *Letters on the Spaniards,* Coleridge writes Thomas Poole that he can "safely refer" him to Wordsworth's pamphlet "for *my* opinions, feelings, hopes and apprehensions."[19] Later in the year, while he is still engaged on the Spanish *Letters,* he recommends *The Convention of Cintra* as "containing sentiments & principles matured in our [his and Wordsworth's] understanding by common energies & twelve years' intercommunion."[20]

It was not Wordsworth's purpose in *The Convention* to make a philosophic analysis of Napoleon's character, but what little he says bears interesting similarities to Coleridge's statements on Satan and Napoleon. Wordsworth attacks the myth of Napoleon's superior talents; he is superior only

in his utter rejection of the restraints of morality—in wickedness which acknowledges no limit but the extent of its own power. Let any one reflect a moment; and he will feel that a new world of forces is opened to a Being who has made this desperate leap.[21]

Wordsworth speaks of the "utter rejection of the restraints of morality"; Coleridge calls it an "abandonment of all principle of right." Wordsworth feels that "a new world of forces is opened to a Being who has made this desperate leap"; Coleridge explains what this "desperate leap" is. The "tremendous principle," the "desperate leap," is Satan's "Evil, be thou my Good" (*PL* IV, 110).[22]

Both insist that evil is inherently weak and self-destructive; on this point it is Wordsworth who gives the details:

It was a high satisfaction to behold demonstrated ... to what a narrow domain of knowledge the intellect of a Tyrant must be confined; that if the gate by which wisdom enters has never been opened, that of policy will surely find moments when it will shut itself against its pretended master imperiously and obstinately. To the eyes of the very peasant in the field, this sublime truth was laid open—not only that a Tyrant's domain of knowledge is narrow, but melancholy as narrow; inasmuch as—from all that is lovely, dignified, or exhilarating in the prospect of human nature—he is inexorably cut off; and therefore he is inwardly helpless and forlorn.[23]

The origin of this melancholy portrait is the situation of Milton's Satan on his arrival in the newly created world. As Satan's gaze alternates between Eden and heaven, his looks are "griev'd" and "sad" (*PL* IV, 27–28). His "domain" is indeed "confined," "narrow," and "melancholy as narrow":

> Me miserable! which way shall I fly
> Infinite wrath, and infinite despair?
> Which way I fly is Hell; myself am Hell;
> And in the lowest deep a lower deep
> Still threat'ning to devour me opens wide,
> To which the Hell I suffer seems a Heav'n.
>
> · · · · · · · ·
>
> While they adore me on the Throne of Hell,
> With Diadem and Sceptre high advanc'd
> The lower still I fall, only Supreme
> In misery; such joy Ambition finds.   (IV, 73–92)

"Inwardly helpless and forlorn," Satan makes the "desperate leap" that proves that "policy" has "surely shut itself against its pretended master imperiously and obstinately":

> All hope excluded thus, behold instead
> Of us out-cast, exil'd, his new delight,
> Mankind created, and for him this World.
> So farewell Hope, and with Hope farewell Fear,
> Farewell Remorse: all Good to me is lost;
> Evil be thou my Good.   (IV, 105–10)

Satan has made the tyrant's choice—to Wordsworth's mind, a choice lacking both wisdom and policy. Wordsworth, therefore, could hardly have shared Hazlitt's admiration for Satan's boast that "To reign is worth ambition though in Hell: / Better to reign in Hell, than serve in Heav'n" (I, 262–63).[24] Satan's intransigence in the face of insuperable odds, which for most of the Romantics became a symbol of courageous resistance to tyranny, was for Wordsworth no criterion of virtue at all. As he states in *The Convention*, "courage and enthusiasm have equally characterized the best and the worst beings, a Satan, equally with an ABDIEL—a BONAPARTE equally with a LEONIDAS."[25]

The consistency with which *The Convention* associates Napoleon and his followers with Satan and the Fallen Angels makes Wordsworth as eligible a candidate for Hazlitt's "political writer" as Coleridge. The atrocities committed by Napoleon in Spain have hitherto been known to men only through the fictions written about "reprobate Spirits":

Merciless ferocity is an evil familiar to our thoughts; but these combinations of malevolence historians have not yet been called upon to record; and writers of fiction, if they have ever ventured to create passions resembling them, have confined, out of reverence for the acknowledged constitution of human nature, those passions to reprobate Spirits.[26]

Although Wordsworth may have "felt a certain faintness come over his mind from a sense of beauty and grandeur" in Milton's introduction of Satan, what he felt very likely was dismay and terror over the perversion of so much that was beautiful and good. What Wordsworth must have admired in the "Arch-Angel ruined" was the Arch-Angel, not the ruin. Once again, as in the case of Coleridge, we learn what Wordsworth thought of Milton's Satan by way of what he says about Napoleon:

In the person of our enemy and his chieftains we have living example how wicked men of ordinary talents are emboldened by success. There is a kindliness, as they feel, in the nature of advancement; and prosperity is their Genius. But let us know and remember that this prosperity, with all the terrible features which it has gradually assumed, is a child of noble parents—Liberty and Philanthropic Love. Perverted as the creature is which it has grown up to (rather, into which it has passed),—from no inferior stock could it have issued. It is the Fallen Spirit, triumphant in misdeeds, which was formerly a blessed Angel.[27]

Wordsworth's poetry provides earlier evidence that he regarded Milton's Satan as a tyrant and liberticide, not a heroic freedom fighter. Although the earliest allusion appears in *The Borderers,* the most significant analogies occur in Wordsworth's characterizations of Robespierre and Napoleon. The earliest text of *The Prelude* (1805)[28] describes an encounter between Robespierre and Louvet, with Louvet playing Abdiel to Robespierre's Satan:

> When Robespierre, well knowing for what mark
> Some words of indirect reproof had been
> Intended, rose in hardihood, and dared
> The Man who had an ill surmise of him
> To bring his charge in openness, whereat
> When a dead pause ensued, and no one stirr'd,
> In silence of all present, from his seat
> Louvet walked singly through the avenue
> And took his station in the Tribune, saying
> 'I, Robespierre, accuse thee!' Tis well known
> What was the issue of that charge, and how
> Louvet was left alone without support
> Of his irresolute Friends.   (X, 91–103)

Abdiel also takes a single station in an otherwise silent audience to accuse Satan "in a flame of zeal severe" (*PL* V, 803–08), although "his zeal None seconded" (849–50): "The flaming Seraph" is "fearless, though alone Encompass'd round with foes," and he answers "bold" (875–76):

Among the faithless, faithful only hee;
Among innumerable false, unmov'd,
Unshak'n, unseduc'd, unterrifi'd
. . . .
Though single.   (897–903)

Changes in the final version of the Louvet incident sharpen the
parallels between Louvet and Abdiel. Wordsworth adopts Milton's
use of an adjective for an adverb: "Louvet walked single" (1850,
X, 111) instead of "singly" (1805, X, 98). He emphasizes Louvet's
boldness; and for Louvet's "irresolute Friends" (1805, X, 103) he
substitutes "men Who to themselves are false" (1850, X, 119–20),
in consonance with Milton's stress on the falseness, rather than
the irresolution, of those who fail to support Abdiel. Wordsworth
also picks up the note of peril implied in Abdiel's attitude: "Unshak'n, unseduc'd, unterrifi'd"; and, just as Milton reiterates the
isolation of Abdiel's position, so does Wordsworth:

The one bold man, whose voice the attack had sounded,
Was left without a follower to discharge
His perilous duty, and retire lamenting
That Heaven's best aid is wasted upon men
Who to themselves are false.   (1850, X, 116–20)

As Wordsworth continues his account of his experiences in
revolutionary France, he once again draws on Milton's Satan, here
to characterize the hypocrisy of tyranny. Britain's entry into the war
against France has given Robespierre further "excuse" for atrocities:

In France, the Men who for their desperate ends
Had pluck'd up mercy by the roots were glad
Of this new enemy. Tyrants strong before
In devilish pleas were ten times stronger now,
And thus beset with Foes on every side
The goaded Land wax'd mad; the crimes of few
Spread into madness of the many, blasts
From hell came sanctified like airs from heaven.
                                        (1805, X, 308–15)

Satan, too, must "pluck up mercy by the roots," must sanctify his
"devilish deeds" with the "Tyrant's plea." The sight of Adam and
Eve fills him with "wonder" at their beauty and grace; he could
"love" them for their "Divine resemblance"; he is not their "pur-
pos'd foe" and could "pity" them though he is "unpitied." But the
exigencies of war require that Satan extirpate his feelings of admiration, love, and pity. If "Hell shall unfold . . . her widest Gates"

to "entertain" Adam and Eve, they are to "Thank him who puts me loath to this revenge / On you who wrong me not for him who wrong'd" (*PL* IV, 358–87). And Milton comments on the "sanctified . . . airs" of this "blast from hell":

> So spake the Fiend, and with necessity,
> The Tyrant's plea, excus'd his devilish deeds. (IV, 393–94)

In the 1805 *Prelude*, the identification of Robespierre with Satan is specific. Robespierre "Wielded the sceptre of the atheist crew" (X, 458). Milton calls the rebellious angels "The Atheist crew" (*PL* VI, 370). Robespierre is the "chief Regent" of "this foul Tribe of Moloch" (*Prel.*, X, 469–70); Milton's description of Moloch makes his name the most pertinent metaphor for Robespierre's atrocities:

> First *Moloch*, horrid King besmear'd with blood
> Of human sacrifice, and parents' tears,
> Though for the noise of Drums and Timbrels loud
> Thir children's cries unheard, that pass'd through fire
> To his grim Idol.   (*PL* I, 392–96)

After 1832,[29] Wordsworth removed all references to Satan and Moloch from this passage on Robespierre's infamies (*Prel.*, 1805, X, 308–15), possibly because Napoleon had replaced Robespierre in his mind as the most suitable heir to Satan's scepter. In fact, this supersession had already begun in a later passage of Book X of the 1805 *Prelude* that describes the consequences to human freedom of France's early forays of conquest at the beginning of Napoleon's career:

> And now, become Oppressors in their turn,
> Frenchmen had changed a war of self-defence
> For one of conquest, losing sight of all
> Which they had struggled for; and mounted up,
> Openly, in the view of earth and heaven,
> The scale of Liberty. I read her doom.[30]   (792–97)

In foreseeing the doom of liberty under the leadership of Napoleon, Wordsworth uses, in reverse, Milton's metaphor for the inevitable defeat of evil; the allusion looks back to the encounter between Gabriel and Satan after Satan has been discovered tempting the sleeping Eve with a dream foreshadowing the actual temptation. Satan makes motions threatening combat when Gabriel calls his attention to the "golden Scales" that God has suspended in the sky as a sign that resistance will be useless (*PL* IV, 985–1004):

                        for proof look up,
        And read thy Lot in yon celestial Sign
        Where thou art weigh'd, and shown how light, how weak,
        If thou resist. The Fiend lookt up and knew
        His mounted scale aloft; nor more, but fled
        Murmuring, and with him fled the shades of night.[31]

                                                    (IV, 1010–15)

In 1816, when Wordsworth hails the final defeat of Napoleon in
his *Thanksgiving Ode,* he uses the figure of the scales in combination with another Miltonic metaphor that marks the final defeat
of Satan in the War in Heaven. Wordsworth explains that, although the nations aligned against Napoleon are equally weighed
in their opposition to tyranny, the privilege of crushing Napoleon's power falls to England because of her long-established
traditions of liberty:

        All States have glorified themselves;—their claims
        Are weighed by Providence, in balance even;
        And now, in preference to the mightiest names,
        To Thee the exterminating sword is given.
        Dread mark of approbation, justly gained!
        Exalted office, worthily sustained!   (155–60)

The last four lines seem to echo *Paradise Lost* (VI, 700–16), where
God tells his Son that he has "ordain'd . . . that the Glory . . . Of
ending this great War" in heaven shall fall to him; and to effect
this, God gives his "Bow and Thunder . . . Almighty Arms . . . and
Sword" to his Son. The "mightiest names" of Wordsworth's lines
may recall that such names as Michael and Gabriel have for the
previous two days fought with Satan and his forces, and their
relative strengths have remained "in balance even." The rout of
Satan and his followers has been reserved to the Son, who has
"justly gained" this "dread mark of approbation" and who later
"worthily sustains" it.

    The *Thanksgiving Ode* provides other analogies between Sa-
tan and Napoleon:[32]

        less than power unbounded could not tame
        That soul of Evil—which, from Hell let loose,
        Had filled the astonished world with such abuse
        As boundless patience only could endure.   (94–97)

The allusion is complex and subtle, for it recalls the Satan of
Paradise Lost who, powerful and triumphant, can astonish Adam

and Eve; it also looks to the Satan of *Paradise Regained* who is himself astonished by the singular endurance of Jesus' "boundless patience" and is ultimately defeated by it. In 1845, Wordsworth added four lines to the *Thanksgiving Ode*, extending the parallel between Napoleon and Satan:[33]

> As springs the lion from his den,
>   As from a forest-brake
>   Upstarts a glistering snake,
> The bold Arch-despot re-appeared.   (145–48)

In the same year (1845), he dictated a note to Isabella Fenwick explaining that "the view taken of Napoleon's character" in this poem "is little in accordance with that taken by some historians and critical philosophers." He expresses pride in "the difference" and trusts that it

> will survive to counteract, in unsophisticated minds, the pernicious and degrading tendency of those views and doctrines that lead to the idolatry of power, as power, and, in that false splendour to lose sight of its real nature and constitution as it often acts for the gratification of its possessor without reference to a beneficial end—an infirmity that has characterized men of all ages, classes, and employments, since Nimrod became a mighty hunter before the Lord.[34]

From Satan to Nimrod to Napoleon: for thirty-six years, at least, despite differences on other questions and the painful rift in their friendship, Wordsworth never wavered in his agreement with Coleridge on this genealogy of murder, oppression, and tyranny.[35] And this genealogy, as it relates to the direct line of descent from Satan to Nimrod, also has its origins in *Paradise Lost*.

Milton's Nimrod is the human counterpart of his Satan in every important detail: Nimrod is of "proud ambitious heart," seeking unmerited dominion over his brothers; he is a destroyer of peace, a violator of nature's law, a hunter and oppressor of men:

> Of proud ambitious heart, who not content
> With fair equality, fraternal state,
> Will arrogate Dominion undeserv'd
> Over his brethren, and quite dispossess
> Concord and law of Nature from the Earth;
> Hunting (and Men not Beasts shall be his game)
> With War and hostile snare such as refuse
> Subjection to his Empire tyrannous:
> A mighty Hunter thence he shall be styl'd
> Before the Lord, as in despite of Heav'n.   (XII, 25–34)

What is suggestive, in this description, of an identification of Nimrod and Satan, Milton makes more explicit in his account of the
construction of the Tower of Babel. This symbol of the excesses of
human pride and ambition has, in very literal terms, its origins in
hell; Nimrod finds:

> The Plain, wherein a black bituminous gurge
> Boils out from under ground, the mouth of Hell;
> Of Brick, and of that stuff they cast to build
> A City and Tow'r, whose top may reach to Heav'n.
>
> (XII, 41–44)

In Adam's comment on the story of Nimrod, Milton completes the
parallel between Nimrod and Satan. Like his prototype, Nimrod
seeks to usurp God's dominion over human life and to God himself "intends Siege and defiance":

> O execrable Son so to aspire
> Above his Brethren, to himself assuming
> Authority usurpt, from God not giv'n:
> He gave us only over Beast, Fish, Fowl
> Dominion absolute; that right we hold
> By his donation; but Man over men
> He made not Lord; such title to himself
> Reserving, human left from human free,
> But this Usurper his encroachment proud
> Stays not on Man; to God his Tower intends
> Siege and defiance: Wretched man!   (XII, 64–74)

This denunciation of Nimrod's crimes, which are so analogous
to Satan's, turns up in Wordsworth's poetry as early as 1796. In
The Borderers, Oswald justifies murder in a sophistical reversal of
Adam's point of view, perverting in Satanic fashion the same
terms of argument for opposite purposes; abrogation of human
rights and freedom takes on the sanctified air of an extension of
human freedom; to usurp the law of nature is, like Satan, to "over-
leap all bound" (*PL* IV, 181):

> Murder! —what's in the word!—
> I have no cases by me ready made
> To fit all deeds. . . .
>   you of late have seen
> More deeply, taught us that the institutes
> Of Nature, by a cunning usurpation
> Banished from human intercourse, exist
> Only in our relations to the brutes

That make the fields their dwelling. If a snake
Crawl from beneath our feet we do not ask
A license to destroy him: our good governors
Hedge in the life of every pest and plague
That bears the shape of man; and for what purpose,
But to protect themselves from extirpation?—
This flimsy barrier you have overleaped.[36]   (1571–85)

Milton's Satan and Nimrod—singly and in combination—provide Wordsworth's poetry, from 1805 onward, with the metaphors for characterizing Napoleon's perfidies. Even as late as 1827, long after Napoleon's defeat, Wordsworth uses them conjointly to trace the origins of Napoleonic tyranny (Sonnet VI, *Poems Dedicated to National Independence and Liberty,* Part II):

Go back to antique ages, if thine eyes
The genuine mien and character would trace
Of the rash Spirit that still holds her place,
Prompting the world's audacious vanities!
Go back, and see the Tower of Babel rise;
The pyramid extend its monstrous base,
For some Aspirant of our short-lived race,
Anxious an aery name to immortalize.

.   .   .   .

See the first mighty Hunter leave the brute—
To chase mankind, with men in armies packed
For his field-pastime high and absolute,
While, to dislodge his game, cities are sacked!

The allusion to Nimrod is explicit, but implied is Nimrod's sire, Satan: Raphael called Satan the "proud Aspirer" (*PL* VI, 89–90); Adam used the same term to characterize Nimrod, "O execrable Son so to aspire / Above his Brethren" (XII, 64–65); and Wordsworth uses the "rash Spirit" of both "Aspirants" to epitomize the true character of Napoleon.

It seems clear from the evidence that as early as the composition of *The Borderers* Wordsworth grasped Milton's purpose in his portrait of Satan; that, while he admired the sublimity of conception and execution of what his manuscript note called the foremost[37] "character, perhaps ever exhibited in Poetry," he never mistook Satan for the hero of *Paradise Lost.* Whether "the Best Knower of Milton" influenced Coleridge's insights into Satan's character and showed the connection between Milton's Satan and Nimrod, or whether the lineage that led from Satan to Nimrod to Napoleon resulted from their joint discussions when Wordsworth was composing *The Convention of Cintra* and Coleridge was writing his *Letters on the Spaniards,* is of no great import. What is significant is that they were unique among their contemporaries in recognizing Milton's Satan as the arch-enemy of human freedom and well-being, not their champion: the prototype of all that is evil, tyrannical, and murderous.

Kingsborough Community College
of the City University of New York

NOTES

1. "The Satanist Controversy of the Nineteenth Century," in *Studies in English Renaissance Literature,* ed. Waldo F. McNeir (Baton Rouge, La., 1962), pp. 197–210.

2. "Coleridge on Milton's Satan," *PQ,* XLI (1962), 504–08.

3. *The Sublime Puritan: Milton and the Victorians* (Madison, Wis., 1963), pp. 61–70.

4. Charles Lamb's inscription in a first-edition copy of *Paradise Regained* that he gave to Wordsworth as a gift; see Raymond Dexter Havens, *The Influence of Milton on English Poetry* (New York, 1961), p. 182.

5. This is one of thirteen interleaved manuscript notes in Wordsworth's hand that I discovered while working at Dove Cottage in July 1963; the volume was at that time on display in the Wordsworth Museum at Grasmere and was removed to Dove Cottage at my request and for my inspection; for a full account of this discovery, see my dissertation, "The Poet's Province: Wordsworth's Manuscript Notes in *Paradise Lost,*" DA 27 (1966): 1343A–44A (CUNY), pp. 1–5. These notes were subsequently published by Bishop C. Hunt, Jr., in "Wordsworth's Marginalia on *Paradise Lost,*" *BNYPL,* LXXIII (March 1969), 167–83, and in *The Romantics on Milton,* ed. John Anthony Wittreich, Jr. (Cleveland, 1970), pp. 103–09. Hunt and Wittreich assign a tentative dating of 1798–1800; for further evidence supporting an early rather than later dating, see my dissertation, pp. 65–78.

6. *The Complete Works of William Hazlitt,* ed. P. P. Howe, 21 vols. (London, 1930–1934), XVII, 63–64, hereinafter referred to as Howe; date assigned by Markham L. Peacock, *The Critical Opinions of William Wordsworth* (Baltimore, 1950), p. 311. For Lady Richardson's report, see Christopher Wordsworth, *Memoirs of William Wordsworth* (London, 1851), II, 454; see p. 446 for identification of Lady Richardson as the source.

7. I wish to thank the Trustees of the Dove Cottage Library at Grasmere for permission to publish these notes; angle brackets enclose deletions made by Wordsworth; square brackets enclose my insertions.

8. Wordsworth was evidently not aware that Milton was drawing on long-established Christian tradition in devising Satan's punishment. See John M. Steadman, " 'Bitter Ashes': Protestant Exegesis and the Serpent's Doom," *SP,* LIX (1962), 201–10; also *John Milton: Complete Poems and Major Prose,* ed. Merritt Y.

Hughes (New York, 1957), notes, pp. 178, 418–20; all quotations of *Paradise Lost* are from this edition.

9. "Marriage of Heaven and Hell," in *The Complete Writings of William Blake*, ed. Geoffrey Keynes (New York, 1957), p. 150; "On Shakespeare and Milton," Howe, V, 63–66.

10. Letter to Francis Hodgson (1821), in *The Works of Lord Byron: Letters and Journals*, ed. R. E. Prothero, 6 vols. (London, 1898–1904), V, 284.

11. "On the Devil, and Devils," in *The Complete Works of Percy Bysshe Shelley*, ed. Roger Ingpen and Walter E. Peck, 10 vols. (London, 1928–1930), VII, 91.

12. See Sankey, "Coleridge on Milton's Satan," p. 505.

13. *Essays on His Own Times*, ed. Sara Coleridge, 3 vols. (London, 1850), II, 657–58.

14. *The Collected Works of Samuel Taylor Coleridge*, gen. ed. Kathleen Coburn, assoc. ed. Bart Winer, 16 vols. (Princeton, N.J., 1969–), VI, *Lay Sermons*, ed. R. J. White, 65–66, "Appendix B" of the 1839 ed. (see n. 2, p. 59).

15. "On Shakespeare and Milton," Howe, V, 66; the "character" referred to is Napoleon.

16. Lecture X, in *Coleridge's Miscellaneous Criticism*, ed. Thomas M. Raysor (London, 1936), p. 163.

17. Letters to Daniel Stuart, December 6, 14, 28, 1808, and January 23, 1809; to T. G. Street, December 7, 1808; all in *Collected Letters of Samuel Taylor Coleridge*, ed. Earl Leslie Griggs, 4 vols. (Oxford, 1956–1959), III, 135, 137, 142, 151, 169; hereinafter referred to as Griggs.

18. Letters to Daniel Stuart, January 3, 8, and May 2, 1809; to Basil Montague, January 7, 1809; to Thomas Poole, February 3, 1809; and to Henry Crabb Robinson, November 18, 1811; all in Griggs, III, 160, 164, 205–06, 161–62, 174, and 348.

19. Ibid., p. 174.

20. Letter to Thomas W. Smith, June 22, 1809, ibid., p. 216. This intercommunion produced not only an affinity of ideas regarding Napoleon and Milton's Satan, but a joint use of a Miltonic prose style to convey those ideas. Coleridge points to Wordsworth's Miltonic style with pride in his letter to Thomas Poole, January 12, 1810, Griggs, III, 273. Southey, on the other hand, found Wordsworth's Miltonic style an impediment to the pamphlet's effectiveness; see his letter to Walter Scott, July 30, 1809, in *The Life and Correspondence of Robert Southey*, ed. Charles Cuthbert Southey (London, 1849–1850), III, 246–47; also Southey's review of *The Convention of Cintra* in *The Eclectic Review* (July 1809), cited in Elsie Smith, *An Estimate of William Wordsworth by His Contemporaries 1793–1822* (Oxford, 1932), pp. 114–17. Lamb, however, agreed with Coleridge on the Miltonic stature of Wordsworth's pamphlet in his letter of October 30, 1809, in *The Works of Charles and Mary Lamb*, ed. E. V. Lucas, VI, *Letters 1796–1820* (London, 1905), 404. Coleridge defended his Miltonic style in his own essays; see his letter to Thomas Poole, January 28, 1810, Griggs, III, 281.

21. *The Prose Works of William Wordsworth*, ed. W. J. B. Owen and Jane Worthington Smyser, 3 vols. (Oxford, 1974), I, 312; hereinafter referred to as *Prose Works*.

22. R. J. White, in his introduction to *Political Tracts of Wordsworth, Coleridge and Shelley* (Cambridge, 1953), pp. xxxi–xxxii, concludes that Wordsworth "adopted precisely this view of Bonaparte," expressed by Coleridge in the *Letters on the Spaniards*, "and was even prepared to attribute to him [Bonaparte] the adoption of evil as a principle."

23. *Prose Works,* I, 298.

24. Howe, V, 65.

25. *Prose Works,* I, 235–36.

26. Ibid., p. 241.

27. Ibid., p. 302.

28. All quotations of *The Prelude* (1805, 1850, and variants) refer to *The Prelude or Growth of a Poet's Mind,* ed. E. de Selincourt, 2nd ed., rev. H. Darbishire (Oxford, 1959); hereinafter referred to as *Prel.*

29. *Prel.,* p. 394, app. crit. D² text; see also p. xxiii.

30. See notes, *Prel.,* pp. 604–05; de Selincourt disagrees with most scholars that this passage refers to Napoleon. With regard to wars of conquest, however, Wordsworth does not seem to make any distinction between pre-Napoleonic or Napoleonic France; see his letter to James Losh, regarding Napoleon, which takes substantially the same point of view expressed in these lines (*The Letters of William and Dorothy Wordsworth: The Later Years,* ed. Ernest de Selincourt, 3 vols. [Oxford, 1939], I, 56–57; hereinafter referred to as *LY*).

31. Raymond Dexter Havens, *The Mind of a Poet,* 2 vols., 4th ed. (Baltimore, 1967), II, 542, also points to the parallels between *PL* IV, 996–1014, and *Prel.,* 1805, X, 792–97.

32. Still another analogy occurs in an "Ode" written in the same year (1816), *Poems Dedicated To National Independence and Liberty* (XXVIII, 21–29); Napoleonic France is a dragon that carries Satan's spear and shield. A MS variant of *An Evening Walk* (1794) that uses the same imagery identifies the spear and shield as Satan's; see *The Poetical Works of William Wordsworth,* ed. E. de Selincourt and Helen Darbishire, 5 vols., 2nd ed. (Oxford, 1952–1963), I, 18, app. crit.; hereinafter referred to as *PW.* For the image of Satan's "sunbroad shield" see *PL* VI, 305.

33. *PW,* III, 160, app. crit.

34. Ibid., p. 464.

35. Two letters written by Wordsworth to Benjamin R. Haydon, separated by some fifteen years, provide intervening evidence of this consistency: letter of October 5, 1816, in *The Letters of William and Dorothy Wordsworth: The Middle Years,* ed. Ernest de Selincourt, 2 vols. (Oxford, 1937), II, 751; letter of June 11, 1831, *LY,* II, 554.

36. H. Buchen, "Wordsworth's Exposure and Reclamation of the Satanic Intellect," *University Review,* XXXIII (October 1966), 44, notes the echo of Milton's Satan in the character of Oswald but does not pursue the specific analogies with either Satan or Nimrod.

37. The actual word in the note is "first," but Wordsworth is obviously using it in the sense of foremost.

THE MILTON OF KEATS AND ARNOLD

Douglas Bush

I

A S REPRESENTATIVES of nineteenth-century attitudes toward
Milton, the Romantic Keats and the Victorian Arnold are of
special interest for several reasons. Both were major poets, both
endowed with exceptional critical insight, and their reactions to
Milton were conditioned by their very different cultural back-
grounds, by their individual instincts and ambitions, and by their
very conscious concern with the ideal character and demands of
modern poetry and with their own artistic and philosophic growth.
While their orbits around the Miltonic sun followed mainly different paths at different distances, they sometimes approached each
other. And the outlook and the work of these poets of successive
generations were further conditioned by the fact that each felt
himself an heir, a not unquestioning heir, of Wordsworth and his
conception of what modern poetry should be. These generalities
include many complications, and this short discussion, in going
over much familiar ground, can only recall, in inadequate and
unqualified terms, some main lines of individual development and
occasional points of contrast or affinity. Keats's case is the more
complex (and sometimes more speculative), but, since his letters
are nowadays so much in everyone's head, it would seem to need
less elaboration than Arnold's. Skipping over Keats's earliest
verse, with its mainly insignificant echoes of Milton and allusions
in the vein of eighteenth-century sentiment, we may begin with
the more mature Keats of 1817–1818.

For him Shakespeare was the universal monarch of poetry;
Milton and Wordsworth were lions under the throne. Shakespeare
was the supreme exemplar of "Negative Capability," of the disinterested creative imagination unfettered by "consequitive reason-
ing,"[1] personal doctrine, or prejudice. Both Milton and Wordsworth, on the other hand, were doctrinaire poets and prophets,
given to proclaiming strongly personal views of life, man, and art.
Apart from his notes on *Paradise Lost*, Keats's most extended comment appeared in his long and important letter to John Hamilton

Reynolds of May 3, 1818, where it takes the form of a comparison of Milton and Wordsworth in regard to their relative "anxiety for Humanity." He is, with apologies for temerity, somewhat condescending toward Milton, whose "Philosophy, human and divine," he thinks, "may be tolerably understood by one not much advanced in years." The comparison includes the parable of life as "a large Mansion of Many Apartments," in which Keats outlines the stages described in *Tintern Abbey,* so far as his own experience enables him to verify Wordsworth: thoughtless boyhood, the beginnings of serious reflection on life, which lead on to the conviction that "the World is full of Misery and Heartbreak, Pain, Sickness and oppression," a real sense of the "burden of the Mystery." Keats's conclusion is that, thanks rather to the general march of intellect than to superior individual powers, the modern Wordsworth has thought more deeply into the human heart than the poet whose Reformation Protestantism cannot satisfy a skeptical modern mind enveloped in darkness and uncertainty and compelled to seek its own illumination.

But this was not an outright or a final conclusion. Keats's feelings about both poets could shift between veneration and revulsion. The obverse side of Wordsworth's humanitarian sympathies was the "egotistical sublime," the confining pressure of a poet who forced his own vision and gospel upon his readers. And against Milton's Puritanism must be set his zealous liberalism and his richly imaginative sensibility and subtle artistry in word and rhythm. It was almost purely poetic power that excited Keats when, in the early months of 1818, he made his first close study of *Paradise Lost.* At the start of his notes on the poem, set down presumably at that time, he saw Milton as a poet who was drawn by his sense of duty "rather to the Ardours than the pleasures of Song," yet whose "exquisite passion for . . . poetical Luxury" produced "with some exceptions the finest parts of the Poem." If these words make Milton somewhat too Keatsian, the specific notes show broader appreciation—although, whatever Keats now thought about Milton's justifying of God's ways to men, he hardly approached that subject here. Among the great imaginative and artistic qualities he praised, with illustrative extracts, were Milton's continual use of contrasts large and small, his "godlike" power "in the sublime pathetic," his wide-ranging empathy and expressiveness, his habitual pursuing of his imagination to the utmost extreme, his instinct for "stationing" characters in relation to solid objects.[2]

The fruits of that admiring and discerning study became very clear in the two books of *Hyperion* written in the autumn of 1818, when Keats was nursing his dying brother and in desperate need of imaginative escape. The theme was apparently to be that of *Endymion*, the experience, aims, and problems of the modern poet, here represented by Apollo; but the earlier "Romance," with its diffuse, erratic mixture of the sensuous and the visionary and its episodes of uncertain "allegorical" import, has given place to a firm and massive narrative structure and masculine strength and beauty of language, tone, and rhythm. The whole is at once greatly Miltonic and greatly original, a world away from eighteenth-century Miltonism. The Miltonic elements range from the debate of the fallen Titans and the "stationing" of characters down to innumerable particulars of image and idiom.[3]

The Titans, primitive, simple, helpless deities, react variously to their fall in bewilderment, grief, and rage; but their debate, while impressive, falls short of Milton's dramatic realism and immediacy. Even the philosophic Oceanus, with the resigned stoic optimism of his doctrine of progress and what seems to be a limited Romantic conception of beauty, lacks full comprehension of the darkened world of loss and pain (if that was Keats's view of him). In general, we are probably less moved by the Titans' woes than we are by the inlaid beauty of the many facets of the "material sublime" and by the majestic rhythm (Keats's spondaic pace is slower and less varied than Milton's). The long fragment, however splendid, was for Keats a tour de force which he could not carry to completion. If falling in love led him into the more congenial romantic luxuries of *The Eve of St. Agnes*, *Hyperion* had its own internal difficulties: Keats had been speaking in a voice only half his own, and commitment to the objectivity of epic narrative and description had kept him from getting into what was, at least originally, to have been his central theme, the experience and significance of Apollo. It was not until the spring of 1819 that he added to *Hyperion* the fragment of a third book, a belated product, it would appear, of self-compulsion. Into this, written in his earlier and softer vein, he managed to force a summary statement (not a dramatization) of Apollo's becoming a god, a true poet, who comprehends, with knowledge beyond that of Oceanus, the troubled history of mankind. Such a humanitarian outlook might be called Wordsworthian, or—with religion left out—Miltonic, if Keats had a thought for the last books of *Paradise Lost*.

The younger Keats, while dwelling happily in the realm of Flora and old Pan, had looked forward in *Sleep and Poetry* to "nobler" and more exacting themes, "the agonies, the strife / Of human hearts." To the end of his brief career he was to remain more or less painfully conscious of the conflict between his instinctive love of poetical luxury and his lofty humane and humanitarian aspirations, which were also instinctive; that is, to be more specific, the conflict between the claims of the sensuous and the visionary on the one hand and those of the real world of Shakespearean and Wordsworthian men and women on the other. A partial change of focus brings Milton into Keats's persistent awareness of his divided self: on January 21, 1818—two months after his exclamation "O for a Life of Sensations rather than of Thoughts" (November 22, 1817)—when Leigh Hunt showed him a lock of Milton's hair and asked for a poetical response, Keats in his awkward impromptu affirmed, for the first time apparently, his imperative need of "Old Philosophy," rational wisdom and insight. But one cannot trace the rich, rapid, and familiar process of Keats's maturing. His increasing concern with human experience, with moral values in life and in poetry, with the sorrow that is wisdom, is signally proved by his coming to see the inadequacy of "negative capability." According to that conception, the ideal poet loses or submerges his personal identity in disinterested, Shakespearean creativity; but, in the parables of the mansion of life (May 3, 1818) and especially the vale of soul-making (April 21, 1819), Keats insists that souls—evidently the souls of poets as well as other men—must achieve "identities" through experience in "a World of Pains and troubles." Thus while he rejected the Christian creed, he still had an ethical kinship with Milton.[4]

Within a few days of the April letter Keats wrote the *Ode to Psyche,* the first of the great series, and some critics see the vale of soul-making behind the concluding stanza on the growth of a poet's mind. While it is natural to link two utterances on that theme so close in time, I cannot see Keats's earnest thoughts about the discipline of suffering in the youthfully lush images not merely of the opening vision of Cupid and Psyche but of the supposedly very serious conclusion. Nowhere in the poem, unless in the two lines on the trees and mountains (54–55), is there any hint of "a World of Pains and troubles"—nothing but images of "soft delight." If Keats's theme was profoundly serious, his treatment of it—whatever real beauties it yielded—was partly self-defeating; and his poet-priest is far from Milton's dual conception.

The ode is mentioned here because, beginning with an echo of the first lines of *Lycidas,* it goes on to celebrate Psyche in images of happy piety (30–35, 38–49) in part adapted from Milton's account of the overthrow of the pagan gods in *On the Morning of Christ's Nativity* (173–80, 184–91). We may assume that Keats worked these in simply because they fitted his idea of providing the late and neglected goddess with proper rites and was not consciously setting up a pagan parallel to Christian story (as Yeats did in *Leda and the Swan*).

There is a gulf between the *Ode to Psyche* and the induction to *The Fall of Hyperion,* written in the late summer of 1819, a year of multiplying triumphs and troubles. In this induction Keats does, with unmistakable seriousness, body forth the arduous process of achieving spiritual, moral, and poetic identity through suffering; the poem is the culminating presentation of the whole complex f divided instincts and aims which had beset Keats throughout his poetic life. But two Miltonic items lead us to a quite unexpected result. On August 14, while rereading Milton, Keats wrote to Benjamin Bailey that he was

convinced more and more every day that (excepting the human friend Philosopher) a fine writer is the most genuine Being in the World— Shakspeare and the paradise Lost every day become greater wonders to me—I look upon fine Phrases like a Lover.

Ten days later he wrote to Reynolds in the same strain, ranking "fine writing" next to "fine doing"; and, this time omitting Shakespeare, he declared that "the Paradise Lost becomes a greater wonder." We note first that, as Keats had done at earlier times, he puts character and service of mankind above literary genius; and we ask whether his repeated exaltation of *Paradise Lost* has a wholly or mainly aesthetic base or whether it takes in at least the ethical side of Milton's theme.

Whatever our guess at an answer, only a month later, on September 21, Keats reported to Reynolds that he had abandoned *Hyperion* altogether. The reason assigned—a reason repeated in his journal-letter (September 24) to George Keats— was wholly aesthetic and stylistic. *Paradise Lost,* "though so fine in itself is a curruption of our Language . . . a beautiful and grand Curiosity"; he now feels stifled by Milton's artificial idiom and wishes to give himself up to "other sensations"—as he had done a few days before in the ultra-Keatsian ode *To Autumn.* The trouble could not have been in the entirely new induction to the *Fall* (1–293), the

Dantesque "Dream" or vision in which the poet-narrator moves through symbolic scenes and performs a symbolic, semiritualistic action at the command of the prophetess Moneta, with whom he has an increasingly impassioned dialogue. This section has been justly extolled as the revelation of a new phase in Keats's evolution, in method, matter, and style: he had achieved an elevated yet unforced, natural, distinctively "modern" manner—"the true voice of feeling," in his own phrase, as opposed to Miltonic "art."

In revising the epic narrative to form the main body of the vision—a significant shift from epic objectivity to more congenial subjectivity—Keats, along with substantive changes, took pains to reduce the original Miltonisms (though he added some, no doubt unwittingly). One explanation for his turning against Milton has been that the old and the new styles did not blend but clashed. Another possible reason for his giving up the poem might have been that, since Keats had had his say, had put his central and climactic theme or problem so earnestly, in the induction, a continuation through the epic story—whatever plot he had in mind—would have had nowhere to go but downhill into anticlimax. In any case, when Keats exclaims so vehemently against Miltonic art or artifice he is objecting not merely to a style but to a sensibility, a total poetic outlook, now felt as alien, indeed fatal, to his own; and that, in spite of his early and recent exaltation of *Paradise Lost,* is understandable. Yet we may be surprised that, in each of the two letters cited, in clutching at reasons for his change of heart, he glorifies his old favorite Chatterton—not his great idol, Shakespeare—as the purest writer in the English language.

What matters most, of course, is that the induction is a confessional last testament, Keats's last, anguished effort to define and defend the high function of poetry and to clarify and unify his own conflicting ideas and ideals, to feel himself, though he is not a simple, silent, happy benefactor of man, at least a true kind of poet, not a sickly simulacrum "Housed in a dream, at distance from the Kind" (Wordsworth's phrase is appropriate here). Yet in this effort Milton is still present, in what degree we cannot be sure. Certainly in the opening scene any reader is reminded of the Miltonic Eden, of the brief age of man's innocence. Stuart Sperry has gone further to argue persuasively that the poet-narrator's attainment, through suffering, of tragic knowledge and understanding constitutes a fall and a redemption comparable to Adam's and Eve's.[5] The symbolic experience enacted is anguished for Keats the protagonist and for the reader far more moving than Apollo's sudden illumination at the end of the first *Hyperion*. The idea of redemption from the "original sin" of the poetic imagination is presented here with so much Miltonic, biblical, and ritualistic imagery that, although secular, it is given a distinctly religious quality. Indeed D. G. James felt a kind of parallel between what the poet sees in the face of Moneta and Christ's taking upon himself the sins of the world.[6] The whole conception, worked out with such intensity, is a natural culmination of Keats's most urgent soul-searching about good and evil in life and in poetry; and *Paradise Lost* may have helped to mold it.

Looking over the short span of Keats's mature writing, we might reach some such summary conclusions as these: that his political liberalism was fortified by Milton's, as allusions (chiefly in the letters) show; that his changing reactions to Milton's poetry were not unnatural in a young poet of his period, temperament, rapid growth, and complete integrity; that his intense and finely perceptive admiration for Miltonic art, during much of his ripest maturity, must have had its effects, even profound and subconscious effects; that in *Hyperion* he recreated many features of that art with astonishing originality and power and at least approached a secular version of Milton's epic theme; that, although the achievement of his own poetic identity proved too strong for continued artistic discipleship, he was increasingly preoccupied with the problem of man's—and the poet's—necessary development from innocence through painful experience and in the second and very personal *Hyperion* depicted the process of a semi-Miltonic "fall" and a saving, if agonizing, illumination.

II

The young Matthew Arnold was much less directly and intensely involved than Keats with the bearing of Milton's poetry on his own, but, as we might expect, he took Milton—with the great ancients—as a prime standard of judgment in his view of modern writing. It was not easy to reconcile that attitude with his Romantic instincts and heritage. Most of Arnold's best poems were written in one decade, 1843–1853, when he moved from the age of twenty-one to thirty-one. For this decade—one of social unrest at home and revolution abroad—we have, along with the poems, a valuable guide in Arnold's letters to his fellow poet and closest friend.[7] These letters, though far more scanty in number and bulk than Keats's, reveal much of the writer's personality, general out-

look, and early poetical creed. In his efforts to find firm standing-
ground in both life and art he is, like Keats, subject to shifting
views or emphases.

Born in the year after Keats died, Arnold grew up into a world
that was changing with increasing momentum. His upper-middle-
class position and classical education gave him cultural advan-
tages, and he was more informed, if not more concerned, than
Keats about the condition not only of England but of Europe. In
his "deeply *unpoetical*" age he was more acutely aware of the
advance of industrialism and its social consequences, and such
knowledge aggravated questions which in some form had often
plagued Keats. The confident, busy world of exploiters and the
miserable world of the exploited did not seem to allow any place
or function for the poet, now that the high Romantic faith in
poetry, nature, and man (not that that faith had been untroubled)
had largely ebbed and could leave poets feeling themselves, not
the unacknowledged legislators of the world, but impotent specta-
tors of inexorable historical process. Tennyson, in some of his best
poems of 1832–1842, had, like Keats, felt the serious dilemma of a
choice between aesthetic detachment and social engagement. Dr.
Arnold's son, feeling that along with the loss of traditional religious support, was preoccupied with both poetry and life. A letter
to his sister Jane of January 1851 gives a significant picture of a
poet of barely twenty-eight who is secretary to a cabinet minister:

I read his [Goethe's] letters, Bacon, Pindar, Sophocles, Milton, Th. à Kem-
pis, and Ecclesiasticus, and retire more and more from the modern world
and modern literature, which is all only what has been before and what
will be again, and not bracing or edifying in the least.[8]

Notwithstanding the melancholy introspectiveness of most of
Arnold's good poems, his critical remarks in the early letters are
mainly aesthetic. He chides Clough for excessive concern with
thought, with attempts "to *solve* the Universe" (p. 63), and for a
consequent deficiency in the beautiful and properly poetical (p.
66). Yet he can blame Keats and the less gifted Browning for an
opposite reason: they cannot understand the initial necessity of
having "an Idea of the world" and are given up to its "multitudi-
nousness" (p. 97); and Tennyson dawdles with its "painted shell"
(p. 63). However, when Arnold emphasizes naturalness, propriety
of form, as "the sole *necessary* of Poetry as such" (p. 98), he goes
beyond the merely aesthetic. Poetry has two offices, to enlarge
one's store of thoughts and feelings and to

compose and elevate the mind by a sustained tone, numerous allusions, and a grand style. What other process is Milton's than this last, in Comus for instance. There is no fruitful analysis of character: but a great effect is produced. (p. 100)

Yet he immediately asks "What is Keats? A style and form seeker" in impetuous excess. Even Sophocles is greatest in "the grand moral effects produced by *style*" (p. 101). Young writers should not follow Keats and Tennyson or "those d--d Elizabethan poets generally"; if they cannot read Greek they should "read nothing but Milton and parts of Wordsworth" (p. 97). Thus Arnold's insistence on the beautiful, poetical, and pleasurable does not imply acceptance of the shallowness or diffuse ornamentation he finds in Keats, Tennyson, and Browning; we recall his comments, in the Preface of 1853, on Keats's *Isabella* and on Shakespeare's sins of style. (Arnold's early severity on Keats was to be later replaced by fervent praise.) If Shakespeare and Milton had lived in the modern world of new thoughts and feelings, "the style of each would have been far less *curious* and exquisite" (p. 65). A summary statement of 1852 reaffirms some of these points, in regard to Keats, Shelley, and the Elizabethans, and adds important generalities: "modern poetry can only subsist by its *contents*," by becoming, like the ancient, "a complete magister vitae," embracing religion as ancient poetry did: "the language, style and general proceedings of a poetry which has such an immense task to perform, must be very plain direct and severe" (p. 124). And, as Arnold was often to say, such a style is the fruit of that sanity in which the ancients were preeminent.

In regard to Milton's influence on Arnold's poetry we are in much the same position as we are in regard to his influence on Keats. We assume that strong admiration for Milton must in various ways have affected the poetic ideals and sensibility of two very serious and self-conscious young poets; at the same time we recognize that both were remote in time and temper from Milton, had very different aims, and in their own characteristic writing were not likely to reveal much clear evidence of discipleship. If the classicist might seem predisposed to assimilate and reflect Milton, his brooding concern with the modern soul in the modern world would not find such a grand model readily "usable." Even on the lowly level of verbal echoes, while Keats from the beginning had many, mostly incidental and insignificant, Arnold—outside of three poems—seems to have only about eight. As with Keats Miltonic influence was almost wholly confined to *Hyperion*, so Arnold's essays in epic objectivity and blank verse, *Sohrab and Rustum* and *Balder Dead*, and the elegy *Westminster Abbey* are his chief "Miltonic" poems; but in the two narratives Milton's presence is less apparent than Homer's, and the inspiration of the elegy is less Miltonic than Pindaric. While Arnold had reservations about the choruses of *Samson Agonistes*, he declared that it was impossible to praise the drama too highly: "it is great with all the greatness of Milton";[9] but neither Milton nor Sophocles could impart life to his own attempt at a Greek tragedy. It is not flattering either to Milton or to Arnold's self-critical sense to call his sonnets "Miltonic" because of their often stiff, angular, and oracular compression. Milton's minor poems in general evoked few references or echoes in Arnold's prose or verse; for him, as for many Victorians, "Milton" virtually meant *Paradise Lost*.

Arnold's view of the epic was in accord with a Victorian attitude which, even if it was not the will of God, he helped to make prevail. To oversimplify a spectrum of wide and changing diversity, the Romantic age had inaugurated two main lines of approach—both symptoms of the decline, at least among intellectuals, of traditional piety. (Both can be identified in J. A. Wittreich's excellent anthology.) The revolutionary Blake and Shelley, making over Milton in their own image, saw him as belonging to the devil's party without knowing it and his hero Satan, despite his faults, as a moral being superior to his God. Such "Satanism" had a long if diminishing life well into our century. Arnold (unlike Walter Bagehot, for instance, in 1859) made no explicit "Satanist" pronouncement, although he could see in "What though the field be lost?" (*PL* I, 105 ff.) a supreme English expression of the "Celtic passion of revolt"![10]

But another attitude, espoused by Arnold, became much more common (assisted by the results of "higher criticism" of the Bible): if readers simply put aside Milton's theology, his avowed purpose of justifying God's ways to men, they can wholeheartedly enjoy a unique masterpiece of style and rhythm and many passages of narrative, description, and dialogue or soliloquy. Some such view had appeared in Keats's letters and notes, in Hazlitt, Leigh Hunt, and Landor. It was to be summed up in 1900 in Sir Walter Raleigh's notorious assertion: "The *Paradise Lost* is not the less an eternal monument because it is a monument to dead ideas."[11]

Arnold's ethical conception of poetry and its effects, which was central in his Preface of 1853, accompanied—or followed behind—his aesthetic and stylistic concern; degrees of emphasis varied with the occasion. In *On Translating Homer: Last Words*, which appeared in the same year as the three original lectures (1861), Arnold affirmed that "the grand style arises in poetry, *when a noble nature, poetically gifted, treats with simplicity or with severity a serious subject.*" But before offering the definition, he gave "a specimen of what it *is*":

> Standing on earth, not rapt above the pole,
> More safe I sing with mortal voice, unchanged
> To hoarse or mute, though fall'n on evil days,
> On evil days though fall'n, and evil tongues.
>
> (*PL* VII, 23–26)

"There is the grand style in perfection; and any one who has a sense for it, will feel it a thousand times better from repeating those lines than from hearing anything I can say about it."[12]

Homer is the "best model of the grand style simple"; Milton—from whom Arnold quotes half a dozen other bits—is "perhaps the best model of the grand style severe"; and Dante is a master of both. The simple style is to be preferred, as "the more *magical*"; the grand style severe (perhaps not the most appropriate adjective) comes in part from the necessary accommodation of sophisticated knowledge and thought. Not that Homer lacks moral ideas, "for what he has in common with Milton—the noble and profound application of ideas to life—is the most essential part of poetic greatness." Yet Arnold had already ascribed to Milton's handling of blank verse the fact that *Paradise Lost* is "one of the only two poetical works in the grand style . . . in the modern languages," the other being the *Divine Comedy*. Shakespeare is our "supreme poetical power," but his every tragedy has passages "in the worst of all styles, the affected style; and the grand style, although it may be harsh, or obscure, or cumbrous, or over-laboured, is never affected." Then Arnold makes much larger concessions. Readers may justly raise objections to the plan and treatment of *Paradise Lost*, and it certainly has "a far less enthralling force of interest" than the *Iliad* or the *Divine Comedy*, yet "it fully deserves, it can never lose, its immense reputation; for, like the *Iliad* and the *Divine Comedy*, nay, in some respects to a higher degree than either of them, it is in the grand style." Here the grand style seems to mean only power over word and rhythm, not "the noble and profound application of ideas to life . . . the most essential part of poetic greatness."[13]

Arnold's fullest estimate, "A French Critic on Milton" (1877);[14]

begins with a six-page condemnation of the young Macaulay's famous essay for providing, instead of criticism, "rhetoric, ... a panegyric on Milton, a panegyric on the Puritans." The last phrase, in view of Arnold's inveterate hostility to the Puritans and their enduring legacy, is a clue to a degree of prejudice against Milton which comes out in this essay and elsewhere. The next three pages pulverize Addison's long and external survey of *Paradise Lost:* Addison, standing wholly on neoclassical theory, does not touch the actual experience of the modern reader, who is "tired rather than delighted" by the poem, who feels "the most languid interest" in its incidents and in "the afflictions and sentiments of Adam and Eve." Dr. Johnson's critique is free from rhetoric and conventional theory, and is often "thoroughly sound," but his judgment was often "bounded" and "warped," not sufficiently disinterested, flexible, and receptive.

Arnold's French critic, Edmond Scherer (whom he knew personally) is all that Macaulay, Addison, and Johnson were not; he has some of the great virtues of Sainte-Beuve and "a much more solid acquaintance with foreign languages." After some deprecation of Scherer's excessive trust in the historical method of criticism, Arnold goes on, through summary and quotation, to present Scherer's main points, with a running commentary.[15] In "Maurice de Guérin" Arnold had said that "no contemporary English prose-writer must be matched with Milton except Milton himself."[16] On the prose, he now accepts, with strong qualifications, Scherer's tribute to the "magnificences of his style," but the phrase "miserable discussions"—which Scherer applied only to Milton's poorest polemical writing and with reference to the jets of magnificence which appeared even in it—Arnold applies to "the mass of his prose treatises." Such a blanket judgment attests both Arnold's anti-Puritanism and, again, his scant respect for the historical approach (though he could on occasion use it himself). He might—or might not—have changed his mind if he could have known the vast enlightenment modern study of the history of ideas has brought about, in regard to Milton and many other authors of the past; indeed notable work had already come from such English pioneers as David Masson. Of course Arnold is, as usual, speaking for the generality of educated readers, not for scholars; but in our time the results of scholarship have, through college courses and books, filtered down more or less to general readers, with beneficial results.

Arnold goes along with Scherer's view that, from the first, "two conflicting forces, two sources of inspiration, had contended with one another . . . for the possession of Milton—the Renascence and Puritanism," and that Puritanism eventually won, at least in the contents of *Paradise Lost,* which, both critics mistakenly say, "are given by Puritanism." Christian theology, especially Puritan theology, is "unmanageable in an epic poem" formally modeled on the ancient epics, the *Aeneid* in particular. And Milton's heavy liability is not merely in theology but in a thesis which does not work. We cannot nowadays, say the two critics, take literally the story of the Fall, yet "the whole real interest of the poem" depends on our doing so. Arnold goes with or beyond Scherer in condemning (like Addison and Johnson) the allegory of Sin and Death as "uncouth and unpleasing"; modern critics see it as a grimly effective example of the way in which Milton makes hell a monstrous parody of heaven. And for modern critics the adverse side of Scherer's summing up is enough to throw him out of court:

Paradise Lost is a false poem, a grotesque poem, a tiresome poem; there is not one reader out of a hundred who can read the ninth and tenth books without smiling, or the eleventh and twelfth without yawning. The whole thing is without solidity; it is a pyramid resting on its apex, the most solemn of problems resolved by the most puerile of means.

Arnold seems to find this a bit strong, but he fully concurs with what Scherer puts in the other scale: "And, notwithstanding, *Paradise Lost* is immortal. It lives by a certain number of episodes which are for ever famous." It

is studded with incomparable lines. Milton's poetry is, as it were, the very essence of poetry. The author seems to think always in images, and these images are grand and proud like his soul, a wonderful mixture of the sublime and the picturesque.

Arnold endorses and expands Scherer's view, the view Arnold himself had long held, of "what is undoubtedly Milton's true distinction as a poet, his 'unfailing level of style.' " (In his essay on Wordsworth, by the way, Arnold sees *Paradise Regained* as "a great poem" by virtue of "the incomparable charm of Milton's power of poetic style."[17]) "His power both of diction and of rhythm," says Arnold, "is unsurpassable, and it is characterised by being always present—not depending on an access of emotion, not intermittent, but, like the grace of Raphael, working in its possessor as a constant gift of nature"—a gift belonging, "alone in English art," to Milton, for Shakespeare has not such "perfect sureness of hand in his style." Further, "as a man, too, not less than as a poet, Milton has a side of unsurpassable grandeur." The elevation which is the great character of his style is connected with the elevation of his personal character; here Arnold quotes, as Scherer had quoted, from Milton's account of the growth of his devotion to chastity, which has his typical "accent of absolute sincerity." This is well said. And we might wish that in this essay and elsewhere Arnold were as charitable in regard to the *"unamiable"* faults of Milton's Puritan and polemical temper as he is in regard to Dante's faults of character and conduct.[18]

In conclusion, while Arnold thinks Scherer rather more given to censure than to praise, he approves as just the verdict that the "fundamental conceptions" of *Paradise Lost* "have become foreign to us" and that, if the poem lives, as it does, it lives in spite of its subject. Neither critic explains how Dante's fundamental conceptions are less foreign.

The next notable utterances on Milton come in the very important and familiar essay, "The Study of Poetry," which, we remember, was designed as the introduction to T. H. Ward's large anthology.[19] Arnold expands what he had said long before about the immense ethical and cultural responsibilities of modern poetry,[20] but in the survey that follows he is much more directly concerned with the artistic power which is the sine qua non of any effective "criticism of life." In the best poetry, however, that power is inseparable from truth and seriousness. As in the lectures on translating Homer, Arnold uses touchstone quotations to enable the perceptive reader to distinguish by experience the best poetry from inferior kinds and not to be misled by either the historical estimate or personal bias. His touchstones of the very best are drawn from Homer, Dante, Shakespeare, and Milton; the Miltonic items are from the description of Satan (*PL* I, 599–602), from Satan's first speech (I, 108–09), and from the picture of Eden, "the exquisite close to the loss of Proserpine": "which cost Ceres all that pain / To seek her through the world" (IV, 271–72). (This last, by the way, Keats had cited in his notes and in a letter to Bailey of July 18, 1818.) As the generally hostile T. S. Eliot said, "to be able to quote as Arnold could is the best evidence of taste," and if his touchstones now seem obvious, it was he who impressed them on the general consciousness. Since he is writing an essay, not a book, his critical remarks are more general than precise. Finally, notwithstanding the large liability of Milton's conception and treatment of his subject, which Arnold had registered in discussing Scherer (and which he was to recall briefly in his last utterance of 1888), it is clear, however little support the critic provides, that along with artistic power Milton commands the requisite "high seriousness." At the same time, ranking Wordsworth next to Shakespeare and Milton, Arnold could say that Wordsworth's "body of work is more interesting than Milton's, though not so great";[21] the reasons behind this capsule verdict, we may infer, were akin to those given in Keats's extended comparison.

Arnold's last comment on Milton, a ceremonial speech delivered two months before his death (*Essays in Criticism, Second Series*, 1888), naturally offered nothing new but emphasized some main ideas we have met in and since his early letters. Compared with Shakespeare and lesser English poets, Milton is unique in "the sure and flawless perfection of his rhythm and diction"; and the "mighty power of poetry and art," "the soul of this power . . . resides chiefly in the refining and elevation wrought in us by the high and rare excellence of the great style." For the increasing millions of people who know no Greek or Latin, Milton is the one English poet who can give a "sense of the power and charm of the great poets of antiquity." The special greatness, the disciplined excellence, of Milton must remain a bulwark against what Arnold had long fought with caustic irony, the philistine acceptance of commonness, the vulgarity he saw spreading over England and the United States.[22]

Keats's reactions to Milton are so closely bound up with his own poetic growth that, whether he seems right or wrong, he wins and keeps our sympathy; and his notes on *Paradise Lost*, however brief, give us insight into both Milton and himself. Arnold's much fuller comments on Milton and the epic in particular remain classic formulations of general attitudes and ideas which existed before him and which he did much to establish as orthodoxy. While his views of Keats underwent a radical change for the better, his view of Milton continued to be in essence the same throughout his life. We may wish that that view, however fine in some ways, could have been—to use an Arnoldian word—more "adequate."

Harvard University

NOTES

1. Keats's letters are quoted from Hyder E. Rollins's edition, *The Letters of John Keats 1814–1821*, 2 vols. (Cambridge, Mass., 1958), by permission of the Harvard University Press. The two phrases are quoted from the letter to George

and Tom Keats of December 27(?), 1817, and the letter to Benjamin Bailey of November 22, 1817 (I, 193, 185).

2. J. A. Wittreich, ed., *The Romantics on Milton* (Cleveland and London, 1970), pp. 553–60.

3. Concrete examples of these elements are in Ernest de Sélincourt, *The Poems of John Keats*, 5th ed. (London, 1926), notes *passim*, and in R. D. Havens, *The Influence of Milton on English Poetry* (Cambridge, Mass., 1922); a concrete analysis is in W. J. Bate, *The Stylistic Development of Keats* (New York and London, 1945). Varying views of Milton's influence on the theme of *Hyperion* and the *Fall* are given, for example, by J. D. Rosenberg, "Keats and Milton: The Paradox of Rejection," *Keats-Shelley Journal*, VI (1957), 87–95; Stuart M. Sperry, "Keats, Milton, and *The Fall of Hyperion*," *PMLA*, LXXVII (1962), 77–84; S. M. Sperry, *Keats the Poet* (Princeton, 1973); W. J. Bate, *John Keats* (Cambridge, Mass., 1963); Brian Wilkie, *Romantic Poets and Epic Tradition* (Madison, 1965); and Helen Haworth, "The Titans, Apollo, and the Fortunate Fall in Keats's Poetry," *SEL*, X (1970), 637–49.

4. Rosenberg, "Keats and Milton."

5. Sperry, *Keats the Poet*, pp. 313–25, 331, 333.

6. D. G. James, *The Romantic Comedy* (London, 1948), p. 150.

7. *The Letters of Matthew Arnold to Arthur Hugh Clough*, ed. H. F. Lowry (London and New York, 1932), quoted by permission of the Oxford University Press. Arnold's other prose (apart from G. W. E. Russell's edition of mainly later letters) is quoted from R. H. Super's edition of *The Complete Prose Works* (Ann Arbor, Mich., 1960–77). Arnold of course figures in James G. Nelson's *The Sublime Puritan: Milton and the Victorians* (Madison, Wis., 1963).

8. In *Letters of Matthew Arnold 1848–1888*, ed. G. W. E. Russell, 2 vols. (New York and London, 1895).

9. Preface to *Merope*, in *Complete Prose Works*, I, 62.

10. "On the Study of Celtic Literature," in ibid., III, 373.

11. Raleigh, *Milton* (New York and London, 1900), p. 85.

12. *Complete Prose Works*, I, 188.

13. Ibid., pp. 189, 211, 144, 145.

14. Ibid., VIII, 165–87.

15. "Milton et le *Paradis perdu*," in *Études sur la littérature contemporaine*, VI (Paris, 1882), 151–94. The essay, written in 1868, is translated, with the omission of Scherer's extracts from Milton's prose, in George Saintsbury, *Essays on English Literature by Edmond Scherer* (New York, 1891).

16. *Complete Prose Works*, III, 15.

17. "Wordsworth," in ibid., IX, 52.

18. "Dante and Beatrice," in ibid., III, 8–9.

19. Ibid., IX, 161–88.

20. I am moved to insert a not strictly relevant note. The first two paragraphs of "The Study of Poetry" have often been misinterpreted by Arnold's critics: he did not say that in the modern world poetry was bound to supersede religion; he did say that it would and should supersede the still current popular and clerical fundamentalism which passed for religion. After all, he had in the preceding decade given several earnest books to the propagation of what he believed to be a valid and invulnerable version of Christianity.

21. Letter to Frances Arnold, April 14, 1879 (*Letters*, ed. Russell, II, 182).

22. *Complete Prose Works*, XI, 328–33.

MILTON AND ELIOT:
A TWENTIETH-CENTURY
ACKNOWLEDGMENT

B. Rajan

To TREAT Eliot's work as constituting in any way a twentieth-
century tribute to Milton must seem an adventure in perver-
sity. There is the indictment of *Milton One* to warn us; and *Milton
One* was preceded by several years of widely admired and therefore hardly inconspicuous sniping with the essays on Marlowe,
Massinger, and the metaphysicals providing typical examples of
offhanded marksmanship.[1] *Milton Two*, which is usually regarded
as a graceful if reluctant restitution for the misdeeds of *Milton
One*, has been described by Eliot himself as not a recantation but
a development of his earlier essay. As a development it is one step
forward, two steps back, to use the title of one of Lenin's better-
known political pamphlets.

Literary history has its ironies, and these may have become
apparent to Eliot as he himself became the kind of institution that
invited deft sniping and expert dislodgment. To say that Milton
wrote no language but a Babylonish dialect is to repeat Samuel
Johnson's finding, which is itself a repetition of Ben Jonson's view
of Spenser. Recurrent conclusions are liable to recur, and a future
critic could say the same thing of that erudite engineer who built
the modern tower of Babel in the Waste Land. That we read Milton first for the sound and then for the sense is an objection which
points disquietingly at the author of the fifth section of *Ash
Wednesday*. Even the resounding statement that Milton's influence on English poetry could only be for the worse might have
seemed uncomfortably pertinent to a man of letters surveying the
embarrassing mimicries of his admiring brood of neither-nor
house poets.[2]

Perhaps it is for these reasons that we are able to discern a
small opening in the Chinese wall of Eliot's defense against Milton. *Milton One* declares that Milton's influence on English poetry
could only be for the worse, fathering the view that the history of

English poetry after *Paradise Lost* is largely the history of the Great Digression. *To Criticize the Critic,* however, suggests that there is a distinction to be made between influence and imitation in that "influence can fecundate, whereas imitation—especially unconscious imitation—can only sterilize." The essay goes on to say that the modified assessment of *Milton Two* became possible because "there was no longer any likelihood" of Milton's "being imitated." When the danger of imitation is over, is the possibility of influence revived?[3]

This may not seem a promising or even a real opening, but we must remember that in a long debate from set positions, even important concessions have to be offered as if they were part of the logic of the position. We must also remember that poets acknowledge each other finally in their poetry and that Eliot's poetry is more generous than the exclusions of his prose. The essayist can not simply declare but propose to take it for granted that "the difference between those who accept and those who deny Christian revelation is the most profound difference possible between human beings." Yet the poet, in an early unpublished poem, can bring together Christianity and the Gita in the presence of that very Emerson whose view of history Sweeney mockingly straddles.[4] The same meeting of East and West takes place at crucial stages in the evolution of *The Waste Land* and of *Four Quartets.* The prose can delineate a position of special privilege, but for the poetry the approach to the meaning passes repeatedly through the confluence of two wisdoms. Milton's stature in the poetic past can be acknowledged similarly and despite critical repudiations, not necessarily as Pound acknowledged Whitman, but as the presence of a writer whose concern with speech and with the structures of understanding gives him his position upon the stairway of knowing.

To understand how Milton is blended into the "familiar compound ghost" it is necessary to suspend some of the judgments to which the prose directs us and to attend to the actualities of the poetry. The *Four Quartets* are poems of place and meaning in which the place suggests what we must learn or unlearn in order to resume our journey to the meaning. In *East Coker* an open field faces the "empty desolation" of that open sea where the mind must encounter its destructive element.[5] The lane leading to the village "insists on the direction," as the Quartets will until the shape of things is known. It is a deep lane "shuttered with branches" and "dark in the afternoon." To remember Samson's phrase at this point might be merely fanciful if the phrase were not quoted in the third section of *East Coker*. Since it is quoted, we are entitled to note that the afternoon is the afternoon of the poet's life and the darkness that of a personal and collective failure.

The waste of war hangs over *East Coker*, the breakdown of the civilizing effort, the questions flung by catastrophe at the endeavor of intelligence. Eliot may not have edited *The Criterion* with his left hand but, as with Milton, the years of involvement brought the just city no nearer. In the face of the mockeries of history it becomes necessary to ask if the gods that fail are the only cause of failure. The collapse of ideals is reflected in a lyric of turbulence in which a destructively organized cosmos mirrors and magnifies the confusion of the lost garden. In the bleakness of self-scrutiny, even the writing turns against itself: "That was a way of putting it—not very satisfactory: / A periphrastic study in a worn-out poetical fashion."

"The poetry does not matter" the poet says. It is a painful remark but creative in its honesty. There are things that matter more than poetry, and it is because of them that poetry matters. A crisis calls on us to examine our assumptions, but the examination should remind us that every moment is a moment of crisis:

> In the middle, not only in the middle of the way
> But all the way, in a dark wood, in a bramble,
> On the edge of a grimpen, where there is no secure foothold,
> And menaced by monsters, fancy lights,
> Risking enchantment.

It was in the middle of the way that Dante woke to find himself in the dark wood, but Milton also, with half his life spent "in this dark world and wide," asked himself if his talent was not lodged uselessly with him. The dark wood is the scene of *Comus* and it is in *Comus* that the Lady is menaced by monsters. "Risking enchantment" remembers the Lady's predicament in *Comus* as well as those "Faery Elves" in *Paradise Lost* whose revels "some belated Peasant sees" (I, 783).[6] Darkness in the afternoon has brought us to the understanding that we are always threatened by delusion and darkness, that the price of intelligence is eternal vigilance. The houses of the past have all gone under the sea. The dance of degree has vanished under the hill. We begin in destitution as Samson did. If we are not imprisoned, it is a complementary fate to be cast loose from the life line of belonging.

Milton is not the principal voice in *Four Quartets*, but he is

one of the voices who speak in commentary on the human involvement, who articulate the relevance of the past even while the
past is felt to be obsolete. The oblique references to Milton in the
first two sections of *East Coker* are now consolidated, as Samson's
cry with its entombing repetitions explicitly initiates the proces-
sion into nothingness:

> O dark, dark, dark. They all go into the dark
> The vacant interstellar spaces, the vacant into the vacant,
> The captains, merchant bankers, eminent men of letters,
> The generous patrons of art, the statesmen and the rulers,
> Distinguished civil servants, chairmen of many committees,
> Industrial lords and petty contractors, all go into the dark.

Perhaps the text gives us an opportunity to meditate on the
distinction between imitation and influence. *Samson Agonistes*
sets in motion many meanings of blindness and of darkness. The
way up is the way down for Milton's hero as it is in the second of
the epigraphs to *Four Quartets* and in the advance of the Quartets
themselves, the movement out of the enclosed garden into experience, so that what the garden means can be found in its recovery.
The context is therefore fitting. The application also fits, as the
catalogue enumerates its Honours List of vanities, not forgetting
in its ironic inclusiveness the author himself, that eminent man of
letters. We can be among the new Philistines, proceeding toward
a carnival-funeral that is no longer heroic, a rite of emptiness without the pretext of a body. Or we can move like Samson into that
deeper darkness which must be lived through if we are to attain
the light. The parallel will outline one's initial response to the
relationship, but *East Coker* has its own way of finding, born out
of its own particularities of loss. We are some distance from Samson when his cry is used to characterize not his own predicament
but that of the Philistines, to suggest not anguish but the ironically
viewed delusion. We should be aware too of the changes of detail
as the transference takes place from one poet to the other. Though
Eliot, in discussing Milton's "vacant interlunar cave," described
"interlunar" as "a stroke of genius," the word he decided to use
was "interstellar." Though he seemed to regard "vacant" as an
inert word neither giving nor receiving life from its surroundings,
he himself used the word three times.[7] The repetition plays on the
difference between vacancy and vacuity while keeping us aware
that interstallar space is largely emptiness. It is a nice comment on
progression in the galaxies of secular power, the well-merited pro-

motion to the long-awaited opening, the hierarchic ascent from the lesser to the nobler infirmity. I should add that Milton's use of the word also has its niceties. It does not simply point out that the cave is, as we might expect, unoccupied. Because the cave is empty, the moon's occupancy of it can be indefinite, intensifying the night's darkness with a desertion no longer reassuringly periodic. Samson himself will speak later of heaven's desertion. The moon moreover is silent. To the man who cannot see, the last hope lies in hearing. We may note (as Eliot does) that it was the silence, not the extent, of interstellar space that Pascal found terrifying. The joint effect of darkness, desertion, and silence is to extend to the utmost of anguish Samson's sense of removal from the creative source. The word *vacant* plays a crucial part in this extension. My intention here is by no means to suggest that Eliot has failed to improve on Milton. Rather it is to suggest how two works of the mind are differentiated, yet vitally connected, on the ground of a studiously chosen verbal acknowledgment. If Milton's presence is to be established in Eliot's poetry it must be within the scheme of a world that is "invented" rather than "collected." This distinction is not taken from unfamiliar Eliot but is made by Pierre Boulez in commenting on Bartok's music.[8]

Milton's work has been specifically present in the first three sections of *East Coker*. The lyric of the fourth section makes no allusion to Milton's poetry unless we take "The whole earth is our hospital" as evoking not only Sir Thomas Browne but that catalogue of illnesses in the eleventh book of *Paradise Lost* which Milton saw fit to expand in the second edition. Eliot's lyric, however, is contrived in a manner that is strenuously metaphysical rather than Miltonic. It would be judging the exercise too harshly to call it imitative in the sense in which Eliot has used and discounted the term, but to admirers of *Milton One* it does make the point that Milton's influence is not the only one to threaten the twentieth century.

The end of *East Coker* finds the poet in the middle which is the beginning: "So here I am, in the middle way, having had twenty years— / Twenty years largely wasted, the years of *l'entre deux guerres.*" That phrase, "in the middle way," has already been charged with echoes from Dante and Milton. But parallels become more potent when the middle once again marks the end of an era and when twenty years are considered to have been wasted as Milton wasted the years of the Interregnum. In the end the waste may not be real, but the expense of spirit for a destruc-

tive consequence calls on the mind to take stock of itself. A decisive frustration demands a wholly new start. The older poet, blind
but undefeated, made this start by giving himself to the writing of
the most sustained and inclusive long poem in the language. The
poet in *East Coker* looks out at the forbidding sea and looks back
at the ancestral migration. Old men ought to be explorers because
it is in the stubborn nature of mind to refuse to desist from the
endeavor to understand. The garden may be destroyed as well as
lost, but if it exists it stands at the end of a journey so that it is not
only found but, as Milton puts it, "rais'd in the waste Wilderness"
(*PR* I, 7), reconstituted by the self-advancing effort. Once again it
is the elder poet whose work provides a paradigm for the journey
and a pattern for the garden's restoration.

Milton's presence in *East Coker* is thus more pervasive and
more deeply acknowledged than the carefully limited concessions
of the criticism might suggest. A meeting ground is created. It is
natural to suggest that both accomplishments illuminate each
other at the point of meeting. It is more important, however, that
both accomplishments are jointly illuminated by the common concerns that the meeting makes them reflect.

Little Gidding completes the circle, restoring meaning to the
destructive reaches of experience. It is a poem of summation and
of transformation, a meditation upon history that takes up the
poem's history so that the images of its own past are "renewed /
Transfigured in another pattern." Its season is midwinter spring, a
detachment into reality that flourishes between opposing states,
pole and tropic, frost and fire, windless cold that is also the heart's
heat. The "watery mirror" in which it finds the shape of things
reflected casts back "a glare that is blindness in the early afternoon." The remembrance of *East Coker* placed, as in *East Coker*,
in the opening section, on the way, as in *East Coker*, to the place
and the meaning, is exact in reflecting the distance traveled. This
is not the darkness of alienation but the deep, dazzling darkness of
the light. Milton's "Dark with excessive bright thy skirts appear"
(*PL* III, 380) reflects the heightened consciousness, the saturation
of seeing. Answering "the glare that is blindness," the dumb spirit
stirs with a "glow more intense than blaze of branch, or brazier."
The euphony between "glare" and "glow" puts before us the very
sound of that stirring, while the word "blaze" carries us back to
that "blaze of noon" which surrounded Samson's darkness and
which is now part of the glow of the awakened spirit. Since Samson's lines now inhabit Eliot's poem, we are entitled to think of

the blind hero's recovery, of the movement through darkness to the meaning, of those passages in Milton which affirm the deeper seeing, the interior radiance of the mind knowing its source. Again the purpose of the convergence is not to imitate or even to emulate. It is rather to suggest the existence of that common nexus of perception and relationship which each poet seeks through his individual language of knowing.

Dante is undoubtedly the strongest presence behind the encounter scene in *Little Gidding*, and both Yeats and Mallarmé are clearly discernible in the ghost's "brown baked features." But Milton is also in attendance at this strange meeting. It may be no more than fanciful to conjecture that the cry of "What! are *you* here?" reflects some natural surprise as Mr. Eliot encounters Mr. Milton on the asphalt of the unreal city. But there is no denying a Miltonic donation in the ghost's description of the gifts reserved for age:

> First, the cold friction of expiring sense
> Without enchantment, offering no promise
> But bitter tastelessness of shadow fruit.

The "cold friction" revives Gerontion's "chilled delirium," the disenchantment proceeds from *East Coker's* "risking enchantment," and the bitter tastelessness remembers the "bitter apple" of *The Dry Salvages*. The final gifts of life are therefore founded upon the previous life of the poem itself. But it is Milton who has in the first place suggested the relationship between error and enchantment and who has put before us the "bitter tastelessness" of disillusion in the metamorphosis of Satan and his followers. Though Michael's remarks on growing old are in the background, it is the shadow fruit turning to dead sea ashes that we are made to see as the primary endowment of age. The final endowment is

> the rending pain of re-enactment
> Of all that you have done, and been; the shame
> Of motives late revealed, and the awareness
> Of things ill done and done to others' harm
> Which once you took for exercise of virtue.

If the first line remembers Yeats's *Purgatory*, the last line, as Helen Gardner notes, remembers that passage in *Areopagitica* in which Milton refuses to praise "a fugitive and cloistered virtue unexercised and unbreathed."[9] If it is Milton whom we hear, we can also recall the ideal exercises of virtue in *Comus* and *Paradise*

Regained and those much less than ideal exercises to which the left hand sometimes gave itself. The gifts of age can conceivably lead to wisdom, but to be delivered from them one needs to give way to their mockery.

The third section of *Little Gidding* considers attachment and detachment as forms of life which flourish in the same hedgerow, with attachment capable of expanding into detachment, as desire is capable of expanding into love. Memory and the sense of history which is collective memory can bring about the reattaching of attachment to the pattern of things rather than the passion of circumstance. Since this, like the other Quartets, is a poem of meaning and place, the meaning of history begins in the past of the place. The poem plays with a not very inspired borrowing from *Hamlet,* banteringly elevates to the status of strife the family quarrels of the Little Gidding community, and then proceeds to consider strife of a more serious kind. King Charles, who, legend has it, visited Little Gidding after the final defeat at Naseby, those who like Laud and Strafford died violently on the scaffold, those who like Crashaw died in exile, and on the other side Milton, who died "blind and quiet," suggest the associations of the place in history. "Blind and quiet" records the manner of Milton's death "with so little pain or emotion," according to John Phillips, "that the time of his expiring was not perceiv'd by those in the room."[10] It also records Michael's view of how death can come to the man of temperance:

> So may'st thou live, till like ripe Fruit thou drop
> Into thy Mother's lap, or be with ease
> Gather'd, not harshly pluckt.   (*PL* XI, 535–37)

Nevertheless the phrase "blind and quiet" contains a residue of loneliness sufficient to remind us that Milton died in spiritual exile and that the England in which he died was ruled by the cause of those whose violent deaths he had earlier sought to justify. There is enough irony here to make us wonder who were the fortunate and who the defeated. Eliot's careful substitution of "fortunate" for "victorious" makes it apparent that we are not to take sides. To take sides is to entrench attachments, to raid the past in support of present loyalties. The recognition has its bearing on polemical positions which Eliot sometimes adopted and for which he sometimes sought historical support. Even literary critics can follow an antique drum, particularly when the message recited over the drum beat is that original sin began with the dissociation of sensibility. If our search is for the rose of the final vision rather than for the specter of a rose, then it is necessary to respond to whatever in the past survives its pastness and contributes to history as a pattern of timeless moments. One man can be imagined as seeing how he is limited in his exercise of virtue. The other sees how he is constrained by following an antique drum. Both men join not only in awareness of their limitations and in a concern for speech which grows out of that awareness, but also in that more ultimate concern for the structures of understanding by which speech is made significant. It is not only right but necessary to the continuities of poetry that they should come to find each other on the stairway.

Milton is alluded to in at least four of the five sections of *East Coker* and in at least three sections of *Little Gidding*. The citation count in these two poems is probably higher for Milton than it is for Dante, but statistics provide little indication of the realities of a literary relationship. It is also doubtful if emulation, the burden of the past, creative correction, or encounter with the anti-self, provide adequate descriptions of Milton's presence in Eliot's poetry. Each of these characterizations has something to disclose to us. None of them fully comprehends a case that we can describe as encouragingly resistant to classification or, if we prefer, stubbornly hydra-headed.

It would be yielding to the blandishments of irony to allege that the Eliot-Milton relationship shows how Eliot spent much of his life fleeing futilely from his true ancestor. Nevertheless, as we consider Coleridge's distinction between the Shakespearean and Miltonic temperaments, there can be little question of the side on which Eliot stands. Negative capability, as Keats defines it—a talent which he attributes primarily to Shakespeare—is not Eliot's foremost characteristic. He inhabits a position, not to discover what it means to live within it, but to ascertain where it leads, or what it excludes us from finding. He is a student, not of the human heart, but of those metaphysical principles in allegiance to which the heart finds its identity. His poetry is driven forward by a hunger for significance, not unrelated to that higher hunger to which Christ refers in rejecting Satan's temptation of the banquet. Like Milton's, his is a talent of intense integrity and creative narrowness moved through its diversified accomplishments by the reiterated force of a single concern. With Milton that concern is the definition of the acts of responsibility by which man constitutes or unmakes himself. With Eliot it is the passage through the unreal city to the restoration of that lost relationship which re-affirms man in the image of the real.

Emulation of the past remains an intelligent strategy when the options of the genre have not been fully closed and the last reaches are still accessible to the virtuoso's talent. The overgoer not only uses but requires the past. When overgoing is cultural as well as stylistic, the building on previous effort, the citation for consummation, reflects a theory of civilization as well as an achievement of language. Emulation is also intelligent when the point being made is that the vulgar tongue is capable of every previous eloquence. But as the creative possibilities of the genre exhaust themselves, as the vernacular achieves its proper dignity, as culture falters in its movement toward a destiny that becomes increasingly dubious even as a destiny, the uses of the past become more variable. They are particularly variable in the poem of self-achieving where the past is invoked, not as a fixed pattern with which one can devise an optimal relationship, but rather as a pattern that can only be ascertained through the evolution of the relationship itself. The manner in which the past announces itself will therefore change according to the stage reached in the endeavor to gain access to it. When the originating experience is that of severance from the source, literary allusion will begin by reflecting that severance in its displacements, its tangentialities, and its intermittent connections. Misprision may well be its natural mode of acknowledgment of the past until the basic relationship with the source is re-formed. As the exploring consciousness succeeds in shaping itself, it becomes possible to acknowledge the relevance of a poet whose account of the restoration of the body of truth in *Areopagitica* approximates so vividly the nature of Eliot's imaginative journey and who, more than any other dead master, resembles Eliot in his response to the language of the past, his multiple shapings of the poetry of allusion. Perhaps it is significant that Milton enters the world of Eliot's poetry only after the existence of the garden has been established not *apart from* but *through* the exiled and therefore resisting consciousness. It is not until then that the pattern of the loss and regaining of Paradise which dominates and unifies Milton's later achievement can be reenacted by his twentieth-century associate.

Disavowals of style are declarations of independence. A poetic accomplishment must feel itself free from the exactions of the past if it is to negotiate with the past on the terms of a poetic community. Harold Bloom suggests that a writer feels compelled

to create and to maintain an imaginative space around himself;
many authors will testify to the truth of this literary version of
the territorial imperative.[11] But when each writer has established
his space, the space between writers bears witness to more than
one ground of meeting or of change. Milton can proceed through
the genres, treating each as a new exploration of a constant
center, because the possibilities of the genres have not yet been
exhausted and because the nature of the core is not in question.
Eliot must not only discern conceptually but establish in experience the principles which shape the body of truth. He does so by
a succession of language acts, each uniquely designed to make
real the stage in the advancing consciousness that it occupies and
to negotiate the right of the next stage to exist. In the end one
poet, remembering a medieval mystic, can say that all shall be
well. The other, as if looking forward to a modern age of disbe-
lief, can say that all is best though we oft doubt. If both proposi-
tions address our sense of reality it is because both have been
exposed to and have survived the destructive element.

In the *Seventh Prolusion* the young Milton, then a university
student, declared that "nothing can be reckoned as a cause of our
happiness which does not somehow take into account both that
everlasting life and our ordinary life here on earth."[12] The statement comes naturally when knowledge seeks the emancipation of
minds that might otherwise remain mired in temporality. But it
remains true when the mind, having glimpsed the eternal, must
return to acknowledge the temporal, not simply as that prison of
unreality which it has been and perpetually threatens to become
again, but also as the surrounding and responsive element within
which we are called on to create. In the final section of *The Dry
Salvages* the poetry for the second time in Eliot's accomplishment
fights its way to the threshold of the word, tentatively appre-
hended as "the hint half guessed, the gift half understood." From
this fragile tenancy of the order of grace we are taken back into the
order of nature:

> We, content at the last
> If our temporal reversion nourish
> (Not too far from the yew-tree)
> The life of significant soil.

Eliot's poetry has been pervasively characterized by the
mind's effort to identify the unreal city of which it is an inhabitant
and to liberate itself from that city's entanglements. It might even

be said that his unyielding endorsement of St. John of the Cross's view that the soul should divest itself of the love of created things cuts into the roots of poetry which require some nourishment by that love. Helen Gardner describes Donne as someone in whom an appetite for life was crossed by a deep distaste for it.[13] Eliot gives us nearly all of the distaste and hardly any of the appetite. His early poetry is ascetic rather than Puritan. When he accepts the "temporal reversion" to the life of "significant soil" he accepts the middle-ground which is the proper place of poetry, "that dolphin-torn, that gong-tormented sea" on which Yeats embarks not reluctantly but exultantly.[14] "Loves mysteries in souls doe grow, / But yet the body is his booke" is Donne's version of the return, a version assisted by his deft use of the commonplace that nature is one of the books of God.[15] But it is Milton who more authoritatively than anyone else is the poet of the temporal reversion, with his succession of quiet closes calibrating once more and yet once more the interplay between the eternal and the temporal, the reality of the illuminated moment and its continuing presence in the life of significant soil.

By the late thirties we begin to see the end of Eliot's long involvement with the poetry of distaste. *The Family Reunion* finely states the relationship between the enduring and what Denis Donoghue calls the ordinary universe:[16]

> I have spent many years in useless travel;
> You have stayed in England, yet you seem
> Like someone who comes from a very long distance,
> Or the distant waterfall in the forest,
> Inaccessible, half-heard.
> And I hear your voice as in the silence
> Between two storms, one hears the moderate usual noises
> In the grass and leaves, of life persisting,
> Which ordinarily pass unnoticed.[17]

The waterfall marks "the moment in and out of time" in *The Dry Salvages,* and the "hidden waterfall" at "the source of the longest river" is the end of the journey of understanding in *Little Gidding.* The voices of discovery are "half heard" in the final Quartet, not in the "Silence / Between two storms" but in a carefully-related "stillness / Between two waves of the sea." These are the intimations of immortality; the point in *The Family Reunion* is that one hears them as one hears the "moderate usual noises," the ongoings of the everyday. English poetry is not lacking in instances of the music of the everyday or of the deeper understandings which declare themselves in that music; but to the student of Milton, one passage irresistibly presents itself:

> Thus with the Year
> Seasons return, but not to me returns
> Day, or the sweet approach of Ev'n or Morn,
> Or sight of vernal bloom, or Summer's Rose
> Or flocks, or herds, or human face divine.   (*PL* III, 40–44)

These are the sounds of life persisting, the reassuring music of the usual made poignantly real by the presence of its absence. When we hear it most deeply it is in and out of time, both human and divine. The delayed epithet, dropping upon the mind almost as an afterthought, is both the last deprivation and the shaping reality. The passage from *The Family Reunion,* it is realized, does not directly reflect Milton's lines. All that is being argued is that Eliot has made the movement toward the life of significant soil which enables him to write in the spirit of Milton's words.

The final stage of the temporal reversion takes place in *The Cocktail Party,* where a *via media* is delineated between the sterile death-in-life of the Waste Land and the consuming life-in-death of the Saint. There are two ways possible, Reilly tells Celia:

> Each way means loneliness—and communion
> Both ways avoid the final desolation
> Of solitude in the phantasmal world.

The higher way is that of a "lifetime's death in love." If the lower way is chosen, says Reilly,

> I can reconcile you to the human condition
> The condition to which some who have gone as far as you
> Have succeeded in returning. They may remember
> The vision they have had, but they cease to regret it,
> Maintain themselves by the common routine
> Learn to avoid excessive expectation.[18]

We can remember Michael's advice to Adam:

> Nor love thy Life, nor hate; but what thou liv'st
> Live well, how long or short permit to Heav'n.
> (*PL* XI, 551–52)

To Celia's question whether this is the best life, Reilly replies:

> It is a good life. Though you will not know how good
> Till you come to the end. But you will want nothing else,
> And the other life will be only like a book

You have read once and lost. In a world of lunacy,
Violence, stupidity, greed. . . . it is a good life.[19]

Milton would probably not agree that the book is read once and is then to be thought of as lost. In the end Eliot may not think so either, if the phrase "We shall not cease from exploration" retains the meaning that the body of his poetry gives it. Each writer must achieve his own settlement of the interplay between the eternal and the temporal, and Eliot's sense of the separation of being from becoming is evidently more emphatic than Milton's. Yet Eliot's lines remain Miltonic in their awareness of a middle-ground, in their somber realism, and in their quiet hopefulness. Indeed, as we reapply ourselves to the last two books of *Paradise Lost*, Eliot's lines could conceivably be treated as a suggestion on how we are to read them, and in particular on how we are to be responsive to and yet not overwhelmed by the weight of woe those final books contain:

                              In a world of lunacy
          Violence, stupidity, greed. . . . it is a good life.

University of Western Ontario

NOTES

1. *On Poetry and Poets* (London, 1957), pp. 138–45; *Selected Essays* (London, 1934), pp. 118, 209–10, 288.

2. *On Poetry and Poets*, pp. 154, 143, 139.

3. *To Criticize the Critic* (London, 1965), pp. 18, 23–24.

4. *The Waste Land: A Facsimile and Transcript*, ed. Valerie Eliot (London, 1971), pp. 110–11.

5. All references to Eliot's poetry are from the text of *T. S. Eliot: Collected Poems 1909–1962* (New York, 1963).

6. All references to Milton's poetry are from the text of *John Milton: Complete Poems and Major Prose*, ed. Merritt Y. Hughes (New York, 1957).

7. *On Poetry and Poets*, p. 141.

8. Sleeve note to recording of Bartok's *Music for Strings, Percussion and Celesta*. BBC Symphony Orchestra, conducted by Pierre Boulez. Columbia MS. 7206.

9. *Complete Prose Works of John Milton*, ed. Don M. Wolfe et al. (New Haven, 1953–), II, 515; "Four Quartets: A Commentary," in *T. S. Eliot: A Study by Several Hands*, ed. B. Rajan (London, 1947), p. 74.

10. *Early Lives of Milton,* ed. Helen Darbishire (London, 1932), p. 33.

11. *The Anxiety of Influence* (New York, 1973).

12. *Complete Prose Works,* I, 291.

13. *Introduction to John Donne: The Divine Poems* (Oxford, 1952), p. xxxv.

14. "Byzantium," *Collected Poems of W. B. Yeats* (London, 1950), p. 281.

15. "The Extasie," *The Complete Poetry of John Donne,* ed. John T. Shawcross (New York, 1967), p. 132.

16. *The Ordinary Universe* (London, 1968).

17. *The Family Reunion* (London, 1939), p. 59.

18. *The Cocktail Party* (London, 1950), pp. 125–26.

19. Ibid., pp. 123–24.

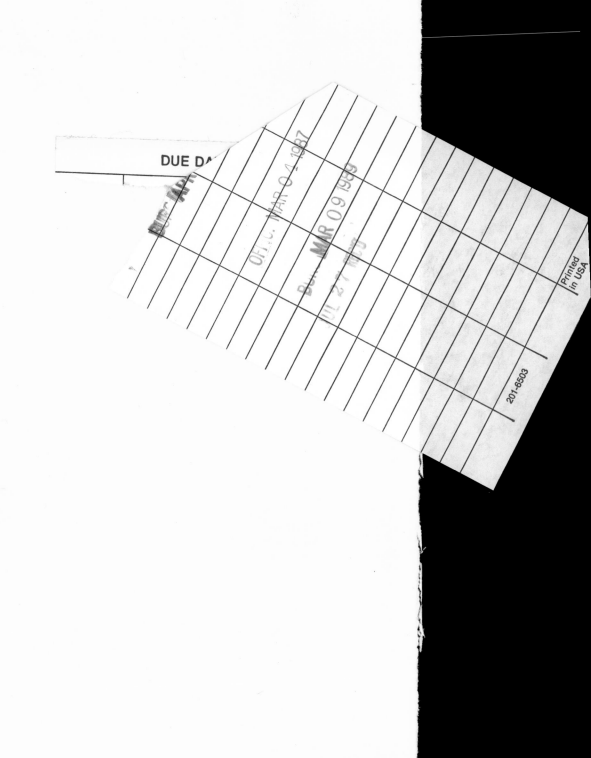

DUE DA

OFI. C. MAR 0 4 1987

MAR 0 9 1989

JUL 2 7

201-6503

Printed
in USA